PHILOSOPHICAL CLASSICS

General Editor: G. H. R. PARKINSON

KANT
SELECTED PRE-CRITICAL WRITINGS
AND CORRESPONDENCE WITH BECK

KANT, _Immanuel_

SELECTED PRE-CRITICAL WRITINGS
AND CORRESPONDENCE WITH BECK

TRANSLATED AND INTRODUCED BY
G. B. KERFERD
Hulme Professor of Latin
University of Manchester

AND

D. E. WALFORD
Lecturer in Philosophy
St David's College, Lampeter

WITH A CONTRIBUTION BY
P. G. LUCAS

MANCHESTER UNIVERSITY PRESS
BARNES & NOBLE, NEW YORK

194863

Published by the University at
The University Press
316–324 Oxford Road, Manchester 13

U.S.A., 1968

Barnes & Noble, Inc.
105 Fifth Avenue, New York, N.Y. 10003

G.B. SBN: 7190 0295 8

Printed in Great Britain by Butler & Tanner Ltd Frome and London

TABLE OF CONTENTS

PREFACE

The great importance of the books in which Kant developed his Critical Philosophy between 1781 and 1790 has to some extent diverted attention from his other works, though some of these are of great importance for an understanding of his thought. The selections in this volume, which have been made by the General Editor of the series, are intended to make some of these works accessible to English readers. The volume begins with Kant's unsuccessful prize essay of 1763, the *Enquiry concerning the clarity of the principles of natural theology and ethics*, in which he discusses problems of method and for the first time asserts the intuitional character of geometry. This is followed by the 'Little Dissertation' of 1768, *Concerning the ultimate foundation of the differentiation of regions in space*, which discusses the problem of incongruous counterparts, and by the important Inaugural Dissertation of 1770, *On the form and principles of the sensible and intelligible world*, which helps to clarify the distinction between phenomena and things in themselves. Some of the criticisms occasioned by the Inaugural Dissertation are included, as are letters to Marcus Herz, which show Kant feeling his way towards the Critical Philosophy in response to these objections. Finally, letters written to Kant's pupil Beck between 1791 and 1793 throw some retrospective light on the *Critique of Pure Reason*.

The Inaugural Dissertation has been translated from the Latin by Professor Kerferd, and the other works from the German by Mr Walford. Professor Kerferd is responsible for the notes to the Inaugural Dissertation, and for that part of the Introduction which concerns the text and translation of this work; the philosophical significance of the work is discussed by Mr P. G. Lucas who, when he was General Editor of this series, planned to publish a translation of the Inaugural Dissertation. The rest of the Introduction and of the notes is the work of Mr Walford.

The translations have been made from the Berlin Academy edition of Kant's works, the pagination of which is shown in the margin of the translations. In the case of the correspondence, the pagination of the first edition has been followed. Kant's notes are indicated by asterisks, and those of the translators by numerals.

G. H. R. P.

INTRODUCTION

I. *Enquiry concerning the clarity of the principles of natural theology and ethics (1763)*

In 1763 the Berlin Royal Academy of Sciences proposed the problem of the application of mathematical proof to the field of metaphysics, as the theme of that year's prize essay. It was a subject that excited wide interest and among the competitors were Mendelssohn and Lambert, as well as Kant, whose essay on the clarity of the principles of natural theology and ethics was unsuccessful. It was Mendelssohn's effort that won the prize.

Kant's 1763 *Enquiry* . . . (first published by Haude and Spener, Berlin, 1764) is divided into four reflections. The first reflection examines the method of mathematics; the second discusses the method of metaphysics; in the third reflection Kant explains the nature of metaphysical certainty and in the last reflection he explains the nature of the certainty, of which natural theology and ethics is capable. In this essay Kant is clearly attempting to drive a thick wedge between the mathematical sciences and the philosophical, in doubtless conscious opposition to thinkers like Spinoza and Leibniz. Spinoza had drawn up a complete system of metaphysics and ethics in mathematical form. (The subtitle of the *Ethics* is *Ethica ordine geometrico demonstrata*.) Leibniz had also sharply divided eternal and necessary truths from those that were accidental. The former express the relations that hold between pure ideas, whether the object of these ideas occur in the empirical world or not. And this, according to Leibniz, is true equally of mathematics and metaphysics and ethics. Because the truths of mathematics and metaphysics and ethics shared the same characteristics of necessity and timelessness, it was assumed by Spinoza and Leibniz that the mathematical sciences shared the same method with metaphysics and ethics. It should be added that it is by no means clear in the 1763 *Enquiry* . . . to what extent Kant wished to maintain that there was an intrinsic difference between the natures of the certainty attainable by mathematics and that attainable by philosophy or ethics. It is true that Kant says at the beginning of the third reflection:

Insofar as one knows that it is impossible that a piece of know-ledge should be false, it is certain. Taken objectively, the degree of this certainty depends on the sufficiency in the characteristics of the necessity of a truth; but insofar as it is regarded subjectively the certainty is greater in proportion as the knowledge of this necessity is more intuitive. Mathematical certainty is of a different kind from philosophical in both respects.

This would suggest that Kant really was maintaining that mathematical and philosophical certainties were in them-selves different. But if one examines Kant's reasons for making the assertions contained in the passage quoted, it becomes clear that Kant demonstrates nothing more than that the *method* of reaching certainty in the two spheres is different and of unequal difficulty. I do not, therefore, think that we are justified in assuming that Kant was entirely dissociating himself from thinkers like Spinoza and Leibniz in this early 1763 work. Certainly he dissociates himself from the view that mathematics and metaphysics may share the same method. The object of the *Enquiry* . . . is to show why this may not be. But we have, I think, no ground for supposing that Kant wished in 1763 to reject the view that metaphysics and ethics were capable of reaching certainty and that these certain conclusions could be stated in *ordine geometrico*.

Kant's concern, then, is only to prove that mathematical method and philosophical method are, as a matter of fact, different. Mathematics frames its definitions synthetically, that is, 'through arbitrary connection of concepts'. Again, mathematics 'in its reductions, proofs, and conclusions examines the universal under symbols in concreto', and that which is symbolised is ignored 'until at the end, in the conclusion, the meaning of the symbolical conclusion is interpreted'. This procedure renders mathematics less liable to error and the certainty of its conclusions intuitively greater. The validity of a mathematical argument can be literally seen. Finally, mathematics begins with 'only a few unanalysable concepts and unprovable propositions'. With philosophy the reverse of this is the case. Philosophy, which includes metaphysics, ethics, and natural theology, proceeds analytically; 'the concept of a thing is already given, but it is confused or insufficiently determined'. The method of philosophy is analytical, and, consequently, part of its function is the task of conceptual analysis. But the analysis of concepts only has significance in terms of conclusions that are characterised by certainty. The end of philosophy is the same as the end of mathematics: the production of apodeictic conclusions. But philosophy has a more difficult task than mathematics; it must examine 'the universal by means of symbols in abstracto'. The symbols used in philosophy, says Kant, 'are never anything other than words, which can neither show in their composition the parts of the concepts out of which the whole idea, indicated by the word, consists; nor can they show by their combinations the relations of philosophical thoughts'. The philosopher must at all times hold that, which is symbolised by the word, before his mind: '. . . the universal must be considered in abstraction'. Philosophy is, procedurally, more complex than mathematics, because it cannot proceed synthetically and is, therefore, more liable to error and capable of a lesser degree of intuitive certainty; it is also more complex because of the greater number of unanalysable concepts and unprovable propositions. In short: 'The object of mathematics is easy and simple; that of philosophy, however, difficult and involved.'

In the second reflection Kant develops in greater detail the theme of the method of metaphysics:

> In metaphysics I may never begin by explaining my object. Far from its being the case that here the definition is the first thing which I know of the object, much rather does it nearly always come last. . . . My duty is to search for the clear, detailed and determined formulation of this confused concept.

But like mathematics, philosophy starts from clear and certain data, although these data are not, of course, definitions. But the definitions of philosophy are arrived at via these certain data, in the same way as the conclusions of mathematics are arrived at via the axioms of the system. In spite of Kant's claim that the methodological rules laid down in this 1763 *Enquiry* . . . 'are quite different from the rules which until now have been followed' his prescriptions are fundamentally the same as the Platonic Dialectic. Both Plato in the *Republic* and Kant in the *Enquiry* . . . assume that a large part of the function of philosophy is clarificatory. But Kant does not deny that metaphysics is capable of reaching certain conclusions, any more than Plato does. On the contrary Kant is emphatic that natural theology, in particular, is capable of reaching certain conclusions. He writes in the fourth reflection:

> . . . the differentiation of a thing from all others can be made most easily and clearly when this thing is the only one possible of its kind. The object of natural religion is the unique First Cause. Its determinations are such that they cannot be easily confused with those of other things. The greatest conviction, however, is possible where it is obviously necessary that these and no other predicates belong to a thing. . . . Hence it is that the absolutely necessary Being is an object such that, as soon as one is once on the right scent of its concept, it appears to promise still more certainty than most other philosophical knowledge. . . . Therefore, . . . the metaphysical knowledge of God must be very certain.

It would appear that at this stage in his philosophical development Kant construed moral obligation in terms of subordination 'to a single end, necessary in itself'. He says,

I ought e.g. to further the total greatest perfection, or I ought to act in accordance with the will of God; to whichever of these two propositions the whole practical philosophy would be subordinated, that proposition, if it is to be a rule and ground of obligation, must order the action as immediately necessary, and not on the condition of a certain purpose.

Although the distinction between the 'formula of obligation' and the 'formula of problematic skill' may sound familiar to readers of Kant's much later 1785 *Grundlegung zur Metaphysik der Sitten*, Kant's ethical thought in 1763 is still teleological, in a utilitarian sense, and his sympathy with the psychological school of moral philosophy is clear from remarks such as 'the faculty of perceiving what is good, is feeling' and 'Hutcheson and others have provided, under the name of moral feelings, a beginning to fine observations.'

By the time Kant's Inaugural Dissertation appeared in 1770, seven years after the writing of the *Enquiry* . . ., Kant's thought had already begun to develop along lines not unfamiliar to readers of the *Critiques*. The 1763 *Enquiry* . . . is interesting partly as a clear example of Kant's pre-critical thought and partly as a statement about the *method* of philosophy, that has become fashionable in this country. It should, however, be remembered that, although Kant says that the method of philosophy must be analytic and clarificatory, there is no ground for supposing that Kant thought that this was the *whole* function of philosophy, when he wrote the *Enquiry* . . .

II. Concerning the ultimate foundation of the differentiation of regions in space (1768)

The 1768 treatise *Concerning the ultimate foundation of the differentiation of regions in space* (first published in the *Königsberger Frag- und Anzeigungsnachrichten*, 1768) is concerned almost exclusively with the problem of incongruent counterparts. The problem is concerned with things that are allegedly identical in size, shape, and structure; although they are identical in all apparent respects they cannot, however, be spatially substituted for each other. The paradoxicality consists in the fact that it is to be expected that things, similar in all apparent respects, conceptually identical to each other, would be substitutable for each other. But this natural expectation is disappointed in the case of certain phenomena, of which Kant gives many examples in the 1768 treatise: spherical triangles constructed on a common base; the hand and its mirror-image; the right hand and the left hand; the right side of the human body and the left side; a screw and a nut that differ only in the direction of their respective threads; species of snail, bean, and hop that are distinguished from each other only by the direction of their respective convolutions. (It is to be noted that Kant does not here separate the problems of incongruent counterparts and orientation. Later, however, he deals with these problems separately in the 1783 *Prolegomena* and the 1786 *Metaphysische Anfangsgründe* . . . respectively.) The paradox consists, therefore, in the fact that an intuitional difference can exist between absolutely identical structures, and it is this intuitional difference which prevents their spatial congruence. Kant writes in the 1768 treatise:

The figure of a body can be completely similar to that of another, and the size of the extension can be in both exactly the same; and yet, however, an internal difference remains: namely the surface that includes the one could not possibly include the other.

This fact is for Kant contrary to expectation; it constitutes for him a paradox, a philosophical problem. The solution to the problem constitutes, also, at the same time, proof of the reality of space.

Kant's solution to the paradox and his proof of the reality of space is expressed in the following passages:

As the surface limiting the bodily space of the one cannot serve as a limit for the other, turn and twist it how one may, this difference must, therefore, be such as rests on an inner principle. This inner principle of difference cannot, however, be connected with the different way in which the parts of the body are connected with each other.

On the contrary,

... the complete principle of determining a physical form does not rest merely on the relation and the situation of the parts with respect to each other, but also on its relation to general, absolute space, as conceived by geometers ...

Again Kant says,

... the determinations of space are not consequences of the situations of the parts of matter relative to each other; rather are the latter consequences of the former.... In the constitution of bodies differences, and real differences at that, can be found; and these differences are connected purely with absolute or original space, for it is only through it that the relation of physical things is possible.

Clearly Kant aligns himself on the side of the Newtonians in the dispute between the supporters of Newton and the followers of Leibniz. Indeed Kant thinks that he has provided the former with a proof of their position. In the passage that follows, which refers to Kant's assertion that entirely separate acts of creation would be required to produce a left and a right hand, Kant explicitly attacks the Leibnizian position:

If one accepts the concept of many modern, in particular, German philosophers, that space only consists of the external relations of parts of matter which exist alongside one another, then all real space would be, in the example used, simply that which this hand takes up. However, since there is no difference in the relations of the parts to each other, whether right hand or left, the hand would be completely indeterminate with respect to such a quality, i.e. it would fit on either side of the human body. But this is impossible.

It would appear, then, that Kant in the 1768 treatise, in opposing Leibniz, was also attempting to prove the very reverse of what he was later to maintain in the *Critique of Pure Reason*. The basis of his proof of the reality of absolute space is the phenomenon of incongruent counterparts. It is perhaps not without relevance and certainly not without interest to examine the way in which Kant was later to use the same paradox of incongruent counterparts to prove the transcendental ideality of space.

Mention is made, for example, in the 1770 Inaugural Dissertation of incongruent counterparts, but their function is no longer that of proving the reality of space, but rather of proving (§15) the proposition, 'the concept of space is a pure intuition, for it is a singular concept'. The thesis, 'space is not something objective and real, . . . but it is subjective and ideal' is proved only later and consequently the paradox of incongruent counterparts is not used here to prove the ideality of space, but only that space is a pure intuition. Kant had, of course, abandoned the theory of the reality of space by 1770.

It is only in 1783 that we find Kant, in the *Prolegomena*, using the paradox of incongruent counterparts to prove the reverse of what he had set out to prove in the 1768 treatise. That Kant in 1783 intended the paradox to support the theory of the transcendental ideality of space is clear from the words that open his discussion of the problem (§13):

those who cannot yet free themselves of the concept of space and time as real qualities inhering in things in themselves can exercise their sagacity on the following paradox; and when they have attempted its solution in vain they can, free of prejudices for at least a few moments, conjecture that there may be after all ground for reducing space and time to mere forms of our sensible intuition.

We find Kant in the 1786 *Metaphysische Anfangsgründe . . .* using the paradox of incongruent counterparts for the same purpose. He there writes (Academy edition, IV, 484):

I have shown elsewhere that, since this difference is indeed given in intuition, but cannot be reduced to clear concepts and cannot, therefore, be intelligibly explained, (*dari, non intelligi*), it provides a good confirmatory proof of the proposition that space does not belong to the properties or relations of things in themselves at all, which would necessarily be reducible to objective concepts, but merely to the subjective form of our sensible intuition of things and relations . . .

Kant's conclusions about the philosophical significance of the paradox in the 1783 *Prolegomena* can be summed up in two propositions: (i) in the case of things in themselves it must be possible so to define them, as objects of the understanding, that we can conceptually construe the differences that prevent congruence. This is not possible with the examples adduced in the *Prolegomena* and therefore the congruence-hindering qualities cannot be objective; (ii) the inner distinction between incongruent counterparts rests on their external relationship to absolute space. They are parts of space and the varying relationship of the parts determines the incongruence of the incongruent counterparts. The parts are determined, conditioned, and limited by the whole. But since things in themselves are neither determined nor conditioned nor limited, incongruent counterparts cannot be other than mere appearances.

There is clearly an incompatibility of purpose to which Kant puts the paradox of incongruent counterparts in the 1768 treatise and the 1783 *Prolegomena*. In the former he claims to prove the reality of space; in the latter the transcendental ideality of space. It is true, as Vaihinger points out (in his *Kommentar zu Kants Kritik der reinen Vernunft*, Band II, Anhang: *Das Paradoxon der symmetrischen Gegenstände*, pp. 518–32*), that Kant maintains in both works that 'the part is only possible through the whole', that physical things are only possible through 'universal space as a unity' though in the *Prolegomena* the part–whole relation only holds at a phenomenal level. In spite of this limited agreement the position maintained in 1768 is clearly not

* I have made extensive use of this work in these introductory remarks.

compatible with that maintained in 1783. Equally clearly the two fundamentally incompatible conclusions are allegedly derived from the same phenomenon of incongruent counterparts. I do not propose to arbitrate between the two uses to which Kant puts the paradox; it seems to me that it is possible that both arguments are mistaken and neither conclusion acceptable. Certainly it is difficult to see how the 1783 *Prolegomena* conclusion follows. Even if it is true that the examples of incongruent counterparts adduced by Kant do belong to the phenomenal world, the paradox of absolutely identical things not being spatially congruent remains.

I have said that I think it possible that both the 1768 argument and that of 1783 are mistaken. The very assumption that there is a problem seems to me doubtful. The paradox only arises on the assumption that, for example, a right and a left hand have the same structure and shape; or, as Kant expresses it, that the difference cannot be given through reason or conceptually. If a right and a left hand are described, it is true that the two descriptions will be identical, but only on the assumption that one is proceeding in *opposite* directions from a point between the hands. In saying this, however, one is already giving a conceptual account of the difference in question. To assert that a left and a right hand have the same shape and structure seems to me like asserting that the numerals 6 and 9 have identical descriptions. Both assertions are partially true but each is also partially false. Kant's problem seems to be very much 'a fly in the bottle' type of problem arising out of linguistic over-simplification; the over-simplification involved in assuming that the incongruent counterparts are identical in shape and structure. Abandon the assumption of sameness and substitute that of mere similarity and the problem, the paradoxicality disappears. The fact that Kant is able to derive contradictory conclusions from the *aporia* considered would seem to confirm this opinion.

D. E. W.

III. On the form and principles of the sensible and intelligible world (Inaugural Dissertation) (1770)

(i) On the text and translation

Kant's Inaugural Dissertation followed his successful application for the chair of Ordinary Professor of Logic and Metaphysics at the University of Königsberg, and it was defended in public in August 1770. The date of the Cabinet decision appointing him to the post was 31 March 1770, and although he had already been hoping for the appointment at the end of the previous year (see *Briefe*, Akademie-Ausgabe, first edition, x, 79) the post only actually became vacant on the death of the previous holder (whose title was Professor of Mathematics) on 15 March 1770 (*Briefe*, x, 86–90). Consequently it is probable that the composition of the dissertation belongs in the period April to August, 1770.

BASIS OF THE TEXT

The present translation is a new translation made directly from the Latin text printed in the Berlin Academy edition of Kant's *Gesammelte Schriften*, Band II (Berlin, 1905), pp. 385–419, edited by Erich Adickes, after incorporating Kant's own Errata as given on pp. 513–14. The Berlin Academy text was based on a copy of the edition printed in 1770 by the Königl. Hof- und Akadem. Druckerei at Königsberg. It has been compared with the Latin text provided by Wilhelm Weischedel in the Insel-Verlag edition of Kant's *Werke*, Band III (Darmstadt, 1959) based on that printed also at Königsberg in 1770 by Johann Jakob Kanter and those variants have been noted that are not certainly mistakes in printing. The Academy edition, p. 510, lists two further printings of the Latin text before its own, namely: Kant, *Frühere noch nicht gesammelte kleine Schriften*, Lintz (really Webel in Zeitz), 1795, pp. 1–44; Kant, *Vermischte Schriften*, Achte und vollständige Ausgabe, Halle, in der Rengerschen

Buchhandlung, 1799, Band II, pp. 435–88. Among other subsequent printings of the Latin text may be mentioned Kant, *Sämmtliche Werke in chronologischer Reihenfolge*, herausgegeben von G. Hartenstein, Band II, Leipzig, 1867. A Latin text is also given with the translations by K. Reich and R. Ceñal Lorente listed below.

German translations (the following list is based on that given in the Insel-Verlag edition by Weischedel—item 6 below—p. 683):

1. Marcus Hertz: *Betrachtungen aus der speculativen Weltweisheit*, Königsberg, J. J. Kanter, 1771, pp. 158. This work by the 'respondent' to Kant's Inaugural Dissertation is to a large extent a version of the Dissertation. It is referred to by Kant as a 'Copey' of it in a letter to Friedrich Nicolai on 25 October 1773 (*Werke*, X, 135) but he was not satisfied with it as a correct representation of his views (X, 127, 135, 139).

2. Without author named: *I. Kants sämmtliche kleine Schriften*, Band III, Königsberg and Leipzig, 1797 (really Voigt in Jena), pp. 1–63.

3. Johann Heinrich Tieftrunk, in: *Immanuel Kants vermischte Schriften*, Band II Halle, 1799, pp. 489–566.

4. Karl Vorländer, in: *Immanuel Kants kleinere Schriften zur Logik und Metaphysik*, Zweite Abteilung, Leipzig, 1905, pp. 87–132 (based on an earlier translation by Julius Hermann von Kirchmann, published under the same title in Philosophische Bibliothek, Band 58, Berlin, 1873).

5. Klaus Reich: *Ueber die Form und die Prinzipien der Sinnen- und Geisteswelt*. Auf Grund des lateinischen Textes der Berliner Akademie-Ausgabe neu übersetzt und mit Einleitung und Registern herausgegeben (Philosophische Bibliothek, Band 251), Hamburg, F. Meiner, 1958.

6. Wilhelm Weischedel, in: *Immanuel Kant, Werke in sechs Bänden*, Band III, Darmstadt, Wissenschaftliche Buchgesellschaft, 1959, pp. 7–107.

English translations have been made as follows:

1. Dr William J. Eckoff: *Kant's inaugural dissertation of*

1770, translated into English with an introduction and discussion, Publications of Columbia University, New York, Columbia College, 1894.

2. John Handyside: *Kant's Inaugural Dissertation and Early Writings on Space*, Chicago and London, The Open Court Company, 1929, pp. 31–85.

French translations:

1. J. Tissot: 'De la forme et des principes du monde sensible et de l'intelligible', in *Mélanges de Logique d'Emm. Kant traduits de l'allemand*, Paris, Ladrange, 1862.

2. Paul Mouy: *Immanuel Kant; La dissertation de 1770*. Traduction, introduction et notes, Bibliothèque des textes philosophiques, Paris, Vrin, 1942, 3rd edition, 1964.

Spanish translation:

1. Ramon Ceñal Lorente: *Kant, I. La dissertatio de 1770, sobre la forma y los principios del mundo sensible y del inteligible*. Introduccion y traduccion, Madrid, Consejo Superior de Investigaciones Científicas, 1961, pp. 178.

PRINCIPLES OF TRANSLATION

In the translation an attempt has been made to follow the principles stated by P. G. Lucas in his translation of Kant's *Prolegomena to any Future Metaphysics* published in the present series in 1953 (Intro., pp. xi–xii). In particular the aim 'is to present an English version corresponding with the strictest achievable philological as well as philosophical authenticity to what Kant wrote so that any philosophically significant analysis of the English text, of the form of expression as well as of the substance, and of detail as well as of the general plan, should yield results as nearly as possible the same as those of a similar analysis' of the original text.

While such an aim can surely never be completely achieved, none the less an attempt has been made always to keep it in mind in the course of translating. Wherever a Latin word has or may have a technical meaning for Kant it is rendered by one English equivalent only and where separate words for similar ideas are used in the Latin the distinction is regularly preserved in translation. (Exceptions are *mens* and *animus*, which are both translated by 'mind', *respectus*, *relatio* and their verbal equivalents, all translated by 'relation'. The translation of *species* is a further exception. The rendering 'configuration' (*Gestalt*) has been rejected after consideration because membership of a species may always have been part of the meaning in Kant's mind— so, apart from non-technical cases, it is translated either by 'specificity' (following Mouy) or by 'species'.) Kant's preference for the subjunctive mood whether required by syntax or not and whether in Latin or German is well known (see Emil Thomas, *Kants gesammelte Schriften*, Akademie-Ausgabe, 1, 517, and Weischedel, p. 684) and this feature has been faithfully reproduced in English even at the cost of occasional clumsiness. Two concessions to readability have, however, been made. Kant's phrase '*non . . . nisi*' has frequently been rendered by 'only', and a number of longer sentences have been broken up into two or more sentences in English, although an attempt has been made to indicate the nature of the original subordination thus destroyed in translation. I am indebted for important corrections and improvements in the translation both to P. G. Lucas and to the present editor of the series, G. H. R. Parkinson. No doubt inaccuracies remain, and for these I alone must take full responsibility. But it is believed that at a number of points it has been possible to achieve greater precision than is the case in earlier translations.

G. B. K.

(ii) *The story of the Inaugural Dissertation*

This is a dissertation about method in metaphysics. (Kant's earliest writings contain evidence of his being concerned because metaphysics was getting nowhere, and the theme recurs continuously. There are several pieces prior to 1770 either directly about problems of method in metaphysics or involving them, and there is plenty of evidence to show that he was firmly convinced, before he wrote the Inaugural Dissertation, that metaphysics would not get anywhere until someone had found a new method. This same point is of course made in a very well known passage in the second edition preface to the *Critique of Pure Reason*.) The remark (Inaugural Dissertation, Akademie-Ausgabe, II, 387) 'For since this genesis, by serving as an example, can help us to secure a deeper insight into method in metaphysics . . .' is to be taken at its face value, or more.

But the 'example', namely the notion of a world, is not an incidental or fortuitous illustration, but is itself no less important in metaphysics than the problem of method. Metaphysics is about the most general things, the nature of things, everything, and the name for everything, or at least for the totality of material substances, is 'the world'. 'The world' is, therefore, part of the object of metaphysics.

The world, as well as being a totality, is also an ordered totality, and further it is an ordered totality of parts. These are the three moments called by Kant *materia* (*partes*), *forma* (*substantiarum coordinatio*), and *universitas* ('matter' ('parts'), 'form' ('the co-ordination of substances') and 'entirety'). Another way of saying that it is ordered out of parts is to say that it is reached by synthesis, and a way of emphasising that it is ordered is to say that there are principles of form.

All this is taken by Kant as given, and would be regarded by him as common ground between all metaphysicians, and indeed between all rational men. 'But indeed the force of the word "world" as it is found in common use springs to the mind of its own accord' (II, 389).

Now the root of all the trouble in metaphysics and the reason why it is not getting anywhere is that the notion of the world is (in the terminology of the *Critique*) antinomic, in that it may involve you if you are not careful (I think the *Critique* would say, must involve you) in the fallacy of a completed infinite. 'This absolute totality . . . is seen to constitute a crux for the philosopher. For it is hardly possible to conceive how the *never to be completed series* of the states of the universe which succeed one another to *eternity* can be reduced to a *whole* which comprehends absolutely all its vicissitudes' (II, 391).

Kant holds that a great part of previous metaphysics, in particular the controversies over atoms or infinite divisibility, over a world finite or infinite in space and time, and over the nature of God's presence in the world and the soul's presence in the body, is nothing but wallowing around inside the fallacy of a completed infinite and it is not to be wondered at that no progress has been made.

The solution to the crux is that there is a hitherto unobserved *dissensus* ('lack of accord': II, 389) within the human mind. (This solution seems to me to have a tragic pathos on a level with the greatest tragic ideas, but I do not think it has ever been exploited by a tragedian.) The *dissensus* lies between the two faculties of the human mind, the sensitive and the intellectual. The Greeks had half got on to this, in their distinction between *phenomenon* and *noumenon* (§3), but 'the illustrious Wolff' hid it again by treating the distinction as purely logical (§7).

The *dissensus* consists in the fact that the sensitive faculty is subject to certain conditions, notably conditions of time, to which the intellectual faculty is not subject. A world as an infinite series completed under sensitive conditions, that is in time, is of course self-contradictory, but an infinite totality as an idea not subject to conditions of time, is not. The antinomy of the notion 'world' arises through not keeping the sensitive and intellectual concepts of 'world' apart. In general, illusion arises and metaphysicians are frustrated when concepts which belong to the intellectual faculty alone become infected with sensitive conditions, through a failure to make this distinction. Metaphysics, being the science of pure intellect (*prima continens principia usus intellectus puri*: II, 395) is particularly susceptible to this contagion. A precondition of progress in metaphysics is to observe it ('Its propaedeutic science is that science which teaches the distinction of sensitive cognition from intellectual cognition': ibid.) and to be up to all the wiles of the sensitive faculty, which can however be conveniently reduced by one principle of reduction (§25) to three subreptic axioms (§27). In thus warning the intellect against the sensitive faculty and disciplining the intellect in its own pure use, philosophy is doing what is needed to make metaphysics possible as a science.

Some other interesting consequences come to light in the process of doing this. There are two faculties, consequently two worlds, the sensible and the intelligible worlds, and consequently two principles of form or order. That of the intelligible world is God and his pre-established harmony (§20, §22). That of the sensible world is space and time, and how nice it is to be able at last to answer the age-old problem of the nature of space and time. They are neither substances, nor accidents, nor relations, but 'formal principles of the phenomenal universe' (II, 398); and so Leibniz and Newton were both wrong.

This in its turn provides the solution of the problem as to why geometry, mechanics and arithmetic have complete certainty and also fit the world. They are not studies of phenomena, but studies of the universal sensitive conditions of knowledge (§12).

This again explains why knowledge of the sensible world, though it is knowledge of appearances, is not illusory but most veridical.

We also have no more difficulty over God's presence to the world, since the world to which he is present is not the sensible but the intellectual world.

But the most important outcome of this consideration of the concept of a world is that, by bringing to light the double origin of some of our concepts, it enables us to recognise the sensitive concepts for what they are and, with some effort, to keep them in their place. Metaphysics, as the pure use of the intellect, is possible now for the first time, since up to now we have not known how to tell purity from impurity.

P. G. L.

IV. Selections from Kant's correspondence with Lambert, Sulzer, Mendelssohn, and Herz (1770–9)

This selection of eleven letters contains some of the most important documents concerning the development of Kant's thought from the appearance of the Inaugural Dissertation in 1770 until the eventual publication of the *Critique of Pure Reason* in 1781. The selection may be divided into two parts: (i) the three letters from Lambert, Sulzer, and Mendelssohn, containing criticisms of the Inaugural Dissertation that had been invited by Kant and (ii) the eight letters from Kant to Herz which reveal the gradual emergence of Kant's mature thought.

(i)

Each of the three letters from Lambert, Sulzer, and Mendelssohn contains one objection common to the other two. Each of Kant's three correspondents expresses his inability to accept the most fundamental of Kant's conclusions in the Inaugural Dissertation. Lambert objects:

All changes are temporally bound and cannot be thought without time. *If changes are real, so is time.* . . . Should time not be real then no change is real. However it seems to me that even an idealist must admit that changes really do take place and exist, at least in his own representations. . . . But having admitted this, time cannot be regarded as other than real.

Sulzer asserts in his letter:

Duration and extension are absolutely simple concepts not permitting of clarification, yet having . . . true reality.

Mendelssohn also finds it difficult to accept that 'time is not something objective and real . . . but something subjective and ideal.' Like Lambert, Mendelssohn argues:

Succession is, after all, at least a necessary condition of the representations of finite minds. Now finite minds are not merely subjects but also objects of representations, both of God and of their fellow-minds. Consequently succession is also to be regarded as something objective.

It is clear from Kant's letter to Herz (*21 Feb. 1772.* 5/LXV) that Kant took this criticism very seriously. He writes of 'an objection that has drawn me into considerable reflection' and says of it that it 'seems to be the most essential objection that can be raised against the system'. Kant's reply in the letter to Herz referred to is substantially the same as that contained in the *Critique of Pure Reason* (Transcendental Aesthetic §7: B 53–4). But this early reply is stated clumsily and without the simplicity, clarity, precision, and sure-footedness that characterises the later reply. Kant's 1772 answer is indirect and involves the construction of a counter-argument; it is clear that Kant is feeling his way towards the elegant, polished, and economical reply in the *Critique of Pure Reason*. It is interesting to quote Kant's later discussion of the problem at length. He writes:

There is no difficulty in meeting this objection. I grant the whole argument. Certainly time is something real, namely, the real form of inner intuition. It has, therefore, subjective reality in respect of inner experience; that is, I really have the representation of time and of my determinations in it. Time is, therefore, to be regarded as real, not indeed as object but as the mode of representation of myself as object. If without this condition of sensibility I could intuit myself, or be intuited by another being, the very same determinations which we now represent to ourselves as alterations would yield knowledge into which the representation of time and, therefore, also of alteration would in no way enter. Thus empirical reality has to be allowed to time, as the condition of all our experiences; on our theory it is only its absolute reality that has to be denied. It is nothing but the form of our inner intuition. If we take away from our inner intuition the peculiar condition of our sensibility, the concept of time likewise vanishes; it does not inhere in the objects but merely in the subject which intuits them. (Quoted from N. Kemp Smith's translation of the *Critique of Pure Reason* (London, 1933), p. 79.)

It is clear both from the passage just quoted and from the letter to Herz, referred to, that Kant's three critics were confusing Kant's transcendental idealism with a cruder, psychological idealism.

(ii)

> ... The works of great thinkers appear in their truest form when the stamp of perfection is not imprinted on them, but rather when they reflect the unceasing process of becoming and the inner restlessness of thought.
>
> (Cassirer: *Kants Leben und Lehre.*)

Kant's correspondence between the years 1770 and 1781 is important above all for the light it throws on the gradual development and progress of the critical philosophy from its seminal expression in the 1770 Inaugural Dissertation to its ultimate fruition in the 1781 *Critique* ... Kant's eight letters to Herz are especially significant in this respect. Cassirer in his *Kants Leben und Lehre*, writing on these letters, remarks:

How this work, in the steady progress of thought, formed itself in him, in spite of all inner difficulties and hindrances, for this we possess in the correspondence, which he carried on with Marcus Herz in the decade 1770–1780, testimony of incomparable value, testimony that must admittedly speak for itself alone, since other information on this period is almost totally lacking.

Kant had written to Lambert on *20 Sept. 1770* announcing his intention of developing the contents of the Inaugural Dissertation into a 'propaedeutic of metaphysics' and of perhaps re-publishing the dissertation 'extended by a few pages'. The latter idea was abandoned, but we find Kant informing Herz on *7 June 1771* (*4*/LXII) that he is 'occupied at the present time working out in some detail a book with the title *The limits of sensibility and reason*. It is intended to contain the relation of the fundamental concepts and laws destined for the sensible world, along with what constitutes the nature of the doctrine of Taste, Metaphysics and Morals.' In this letter we find Kant making the important distinction 'between that which rests on subjective principles of the faculties of the human soul . . . and that which goes directly to its objects'. The importance of the two letters from Lambert and Mendelssohn is emphasised but it is only in the next letter that Kant ventures a reply, the reply discussed in (i) above.

In this second letter to Herz of *21 Feb. 1772* (*5*/LXV) Kant gives us more detailed information about the 'project of a work which could be entitled *The limits of sensibility and reason* . . . conceived . . . as having two parts, a theoretical and a practical.' It is clear from Kant's later remarks that he is no longer working on the 'doctrine of Taste . . . and Morals' but is primarily concerned with the theoretical part.

I am now in the position to present a critique of pure reason, containing the nature both of theoretical as well as of practical knowledge, insofar as it is purely intellectual. I shall first of all elaborate the first part containing the sources of metaphysics, its method and limits. . . . As far as the first part is concerned, I shall publish within about three months.

Philosophically this is the most important of Kant's eight letters to Herz. Cassirer remarks that with this letter the Copernican Revolution in philosophy was completed. Kant's attention is now clearly and emphatically concentrated on the problem of the relation of representation and object. Kant is himself aware of having made a significant advance in his researches.

While I was thinking out the full extent of the theoretical part

... I noticed that I was still lacking something essential ... which constituted, indeed, the key to the whole secret, the key to metaphysics which until then had remained hidden to itself. I asked myself namely: on what basis rests the relation to the object of that which in ourselves we call representation?

Kant rejects both the view that the representation causes the object and the converse view that the object causes the representation; but he also expresses dissatisfaction with the solution offered in the Inaugural Dissertation that 'sensible representations represent things as they appear; the intellectual representations represent them as they are.' The subjectivity not only of the sensibility but also of the understanding begins now to be more clearly maintained. It is true both of the forms of pure intuition and of the concepts of the understanding that they are valid, not because they represent the world of objects in themselves, but because they are the necessary conditions of our experience.

Kant's expectation of publishing 'within about three months' the first part of the work referred to in the above two letters was not, of course, realised. Over a year and a half later we find Kant writing to Nicolai on *25 Oct. 1773* and announcing that his 'present work' would appear 'shortly'. He refers to his work as 'transcendental philosophy, which is in fact a critique of pure reason'. Towards the end of the same year we find Kant making his excuses to Herz (*6/*LXXI):

... since I have come so far in my intention of remodelling a branch of learning so long worked in vain by half the philosophical world ... I am now sticking stubbornly to my intention of not allowing myself to be led astray by vanity of authorship, into seeking fame in an easier and better liked field, before I have levelled my thorny and hard plot and freed it for general cultivation.

In this letter Kant speaks of 'the hope of delivering the completed work by Easter' or 'almost certainly a short time after Easter'.

For many of Kant's colleagues and friends this intention must have been unknown; many of his friends can only have been aware of Kant's continuing silence. Lavater, for example, protests in a letter of *8 Feb. 1774*, '. . . Have you, then, died to the world? Why do so many write who cannot write,—and you not, who can write so excellently? Why do you maintain silence? . . . I will not praise you,—but tell me, why are you silent? or far rather, tell me that you intend to speak.' It is clear from Kant's next letter to Herz, almost two years later, written on *24 Nov. 1776* (7/CI), that Lavater was not alone in his complaints: 'I receive rebukes from all sides', admits Kant, 'because of the inactivity into which I seem long to have fallen.' And yet this period of apparent inactivity had in fact been one of persistent and systematic work; material had been amassing and the summer of 1775 had seen the solution to the difficulties that had remained. The work is one of completion rather than of further research. Kant refers to his own work as 'a critique, a discipline, a canon, an architectonic of pure reason'. Perhaps Kant has grown realistic about his ability to realise his own expectations and doubtful about his capacity to bring his work to completion. He now expresses himself in negative terms: 'I do not expect to be through with this work before next Easter and I intend to devote part of next summer to this purpose, assuming that my continually interrupted health permits me to work.' But the autumn of 1777 is already approaching and we find Kant writing to Herz in a letter, not included in this selection, of *20 Aug. 1777* as follows: 'What I call the critique of pure reason lies like a stone in the way of completing this work. I am now completely occupied with the removing of this difficulty and I hope to finish with it this winter.' Had Kant's expectation fulfilled itself the work would have appeared in time for the Easter Book Fair, 1778. Like his earlier expectations this one was also not realised.

Kant's frequently repeated promises and continually renewed expressions of intention seem to have given rise to rumours that some pages of the work were already at the printers. This rumour is denied by Kant in his next letter to Herz on *8 April 1778* (*8*/cxxı). He adds 'Should I pass this summer in tolerable health I think I should be able to communicate the promised work to the public'. A theme that recurs more and more frequently in the letters of this period is that of Kant's fragile health. In his letter of *28 Aug. 1778* (*9*/cxxvıı) bad health is blamed for the continual delay: 'Without this hindrance my little projects . . . would long have reached completion.' He expects to have the work ready 'quite soon now'.

In fact almost two years more were to elapse before Kant is finally able definitely to announce the appearance of the long awaited, frequently promised, but continually postponed work. In a famous letter to Herz of *1 May 1781*, not included in the selection, Kant writes:

At this Easter Book Fair a work of mine will be published under the title *Critique of Pure Reason*. This book contains the product of all the many investigations that started from the concepts which we disputed about under the name of the *mundi sensibilis* and *intelligibilis*.

In letters written to Mendelssohn and Garve Kant describes how the reflections over a period of at least twelve years were committed to writing 'within about four to five months'. It is clear that Kant was finally induced to give the product of his twelve years' reflection, not from the conviction that he could no longer perfect what he had to say, but rather from the ever-increasing fear that 'the threads spun so finely by the Parcae' would finally be cut and the opportunity of communicating his ideas lost for ever.

V. Selections from Kant's correspondence with Beck (1791–3)

The Kant-Beck Correspondence is constituted by twenty-five letters, of which seventeen were written by Beck to

Kant between the years 1789 and 1797, and which were first published by Reicke as the appendix to his 1885 lecture *Aus Kants Briefwechsel*. The remaining eight letters were written by Kant to Beck between 1791 and 1793 and are the eight letters contained in this selection. They were first discovered in the Rostock Library and then published by Wilhelm Dilthey in 1889 in his paper *Die Rostocker Kant-handschriften*. (This paper is contained in the *Archiv für die Geschichte der Philosophie*, 1889, II, xxxi: cf. *Wilhelm Diltheys Gesammelte Schriften*, Vol. IV (Leipzig and Berlin, 1925), pp. 310 ff. The substance of these introductory remarks is largely derived from this important essay, which is not easily accessible to English readers.) The letters between 1791 and 1793 form a continuous series. Because Kant's eight letters are part of an exchange of letters they must remain only partially intelligible so long as Beck's side of the correspondence remains an unknown quantity. I propose, therefore, in these introductory remarks, to say something about the relevant letters from Beck. The following is the complete list of letters which make up the continuous correspondence (Kant's replies are in the right hand column):

    (i) 19 April 1791 —9 May 1791
    (ii) 1 June 1791 —27 Sept. 1791
    (iii) 6 Oct. 1791 —2 Nov. 1791
    (iv) 11 Nov. 1791 —9 Dec. 1791 (lost)
                      20 Jan. 1792
    (v) 31 May 1792 —3 July 1792
    (vi) 8 Sept. 1792 —16 Oct. 1792
    (vii) 10 Nov. 1792 —4 Dec. 1792
    (viii) 30 Apr. 1793 —18 Aug. 1793

The first of Beck's letters to Kant of *19 April 1791* was written from Halle where Beck had completed his *Habilita-tionsschrift* on Taylor's Theory. Having studied at Königsberg, Beck had gone first to Halle and then to Leipzig where Platner, one of Kant's most famous opponents, to whom Beck refers contemptuously as 'that pitiful man', held the chair of philosophy. Beck disliked Leipzig and returned to Halle where he found support in the Professor of Mathematics, Klügel. In addition Jacob, an early and enthusiastic supporter of Kant, had become *Ordinarius* for philosophy there. It was Jacob who obtained a position for Beck at the Old Lutheran Gymnasium in Halle. It is to this that Kant refers in his reply of *9 May 1791*, the first of Kant's letters in this selection. Beck answers on *1 June 1791* informing Kant that he is holding lectures for 'a few non-paying students' but adds that he is by 'no means disheartened by this unpromising beginning'. Kant's letter has encouraged him, but the literary situation in Halle, about which Kant had enquired, is not one that affords Beck any particular pleasure. Beck also informs Kant that Hartknoch, the publisher, had written to him about the possibility of a Latin selection from Kant's critical writings. Beck had written to Hartknoch explaining his inability to be of any help but at the same time he took advantage of the occasion to express his readiness to write something either on Reinhold's Theory of the Faculty of Representation or on a comparison of the Humean and Kantian philosophy. In Kant's reply it is clear that Hartknoch had also approached Kant himself about the possibility of someone's doing a selection from the critical writings, presumably in German this time, since Kant suggested Beck's name. The matter is discussed by Kant in the letter of *27 Sept. 1791* (*13*/CDLVII). Thus it was that Beck started work on his monumental *Erläuternder Auszug aus Kants kritischen Schriften*, the first volume of which was to appear in 1793. But at the same time Beck had started work on his essay against Reinhold, which was intended to demonstrate the truth of Kant's *Critique* and the essential worthlessness of Reinhold's theory. Kant had expressed himself very coolly about the Reinhold project.

Beck replies to Kant's letter on *6 Oct. 1791*, accompanying his letter with a sample of his essay against Reinhold. Beck, in accordance with Kant's wish, promises to omit all that could be offensive to Reinhold. He also expresses his intention of going ahead with the *Auszug* but asks Kant to act as his protector against Kant's colleague Kraus, who seems to have been notorious for the severity of his criticisms. It is with reference to this request that Kant jokingly concludes his next letter on *2 Nov. 1791* (14/CDLXIV), the letter in which he also expresses something almost amounting to displeasure, certainly disappointment, that Beck should have chosen to write against Reinhold, rather than to follow Kant's advice and make his philosophical debut with a comparative study of the thought of Hume and himself.

In Beck's next letter of *11 Nov. 1791* we find that Beck has dropped the Reinhold project. It had become clear to him that a polemic against Reinhold would have little or no public; perhaps, also, he had become convinced that Reinhold's thought was not capable of clear exposition because of its own intrinsic obscurity, as Kant had himself objected; in addition Beck must have been aware that such a polemic would place Kant in a highly embarrassing position, since both Beck and Reinhold were personal friends of Kant. At any rate the project was abandoned and Beck devoted himself almost exclusively to Kant's thought. In this letter Beck lays before Kant his difficulties about a point 'which was to definitively determine his whole conception of the critique of pure reason' (Dilthey). In the first volume of his *Auszug* he writes:

I have tried to think myself into the spirit of the critical philosophy. This was a matter of several years, having found it, along with mathematics, the best companion of my life. In this way I have made the course of the critique into my own mode of thought, as it were, and I have learned to express the thoughts of another as if they were my own.

Dilthey remarks in the paper referred to above:

He thus tries to translate Kant's transcendental philosophy into concepts that are entirely consistent with each other and that are never misleading. He attempts so to determine the concepts initially needed by the critique, that they include nothing that has later to be established. Thus arises . . . the definition of intuition as an objective representation, thoroughly determined with respect to a datum.

Kant's first reply to this important discussion, written on *9 Dec. 1791*, has unfortunately been lost. It would appear, however, that Kant's next letter of *20 Jan. 1792* (*15*/CDLXVIII) contains the substance of the earlier reply. Beck's difficulties and his proposed definition of the concept of intuition are discussed by Kant at considerable length.

Beck's answer followed on *31 May 1792*. The *Critique* regards intuition as representation related immediately to an object; but since the objective character of intuition arises from the application of the categories to intuition, the objective representation can only appear in the Transcendental Logic. Consequently a definition of intuition must be discovered which dispenses with the characteristic of its relation to the object. Intuition is, accordingly, defined by Beck as 'a representation completely determined in respect to the multiplex'. Kant's next letter, written on *3 July 1792* (*16*/CDLXXXVIII), discusses Beck's definition. On *8 Sept. 1792* Beck enclosed with his letter the manuscript of the first part of his *Auszug* from the *Critique of Pure Reason* extending as far as the Transcendental Dialectic and it is on this part of his exposition that Beck is especially anxious to hear Kant's opinion. By an oversight Kant returned the manuscript a month early without having given himself sufficient time to examine the whole of the exposition so far prepared by Beck. This is explained by Kant in his next letter of *16 Oct. 1792* (*17*/DIV). He expresses his willingness to look through the not yet examined passages if a transcription of the relevant part is sent to him.

Accordingly Beck encloses with his letter of *10 Nov. 1792* a transcription of the pages concerned. Beck includes certain miscellaneous items of news. Garve, for example, was recently in Halle and had had a conversation with Eberhard about the critical philosophy, in the course of which

Garve asserted that no distinction was to be made between Berkeleyan and Kantian Idealism. In his reply to this criticism, written *4 Dec. 1792* (*18*/DXVI), Kant dismisses the suggestion as 'not deserving the least attention'. It is in this letter that Kant writes for the first time of the essay originally intended to be the introduction to the *Critique of Judgement* upon which Beck was now working. Kant promises to send the until then unused manuscript to Beck, for him to make what use he wished of it. Beck's next letter, and the last one relevant to this selection, followed on *30 April 1793*. By this time the first volume of the *Erläuternder Auszug . . .* had appeared. He had covered the two Critiques and was now engaged on the *Critique of Judgement*. He reminds Kant of his promise to send the unused introduction to the *Critique of Judgement*. The last of Kant's letters in this selection, written on *18 Aug. 1793*, (*19*/DLI), constitutes Kant's reply to the last-mentioned letter of Beck. With it Kant encloses the promised manuscript, from which Beck published an excerpt in the second volume of his *Erläuternder Auszug* which appeared in 1794.

D. E. W.

TRANSLATIONS

[I]

Enquiry concerning the Clarity of
the Principles of Natural Theology
and Ethics.

being an answer to the question
proposed by the Berlin Royal
Academy of Sciences for the year
1763.

Indeed these small clues
are sufficient for a wise
mind; by their means you
will be enabled to infer
the rest with clarity . . .

I

Enquiry concerning the clarity of the principles of natural
theology and ethics

INTRODUCTION

The question proposed is of the kind whose fitting solution results in higher philosophy necessarily receiving a definite shape. Once the method is firmly established in accordance with which the highest possible degree of certainty in this kind of knowledge is achievable, and once the nature of this conviction is well understood, the eternal instability of opinions and particular sects is of necessity replaced by an immutable prescription about teaching method, which unites thinking minds to one and the same kind of effort. In the same way, *Newton's* method in natural science changed the license of physical hypotheses into an indubitable procedure based on experience and geometry. But what method should this treatise—which is to show the true degree of certainty achievable in metaphysics, along with the path by which it is to be reached—what method should this treatise itself have? If this treatise is a piece of metaphysics, everything is lost; its judgement is just as inconclusive as the science itself had been until then—the science which had hoped to receive some standing and stability through this paper. I will, therefore, see that the whole content of my treatise is indubitable empirical propositions and consequences drawn immediately from them. I will rely neither on the doctrines of philosophers, the uncertainty of which is the occasion of the present exercise, nor will I rely on definitions which are so often misleading. The method I shall use will be simple and

5

cautious. Some uncertainties may still be found, but these will be of the kind used only for clarification, not proof.

II 276

FIRST REFLECTION

A general comparison of the manner of achieving certainty in mathematical knowledge with the manner of achieving certainty in philosophical knowledge

§1

Mathematics reaches all its definitions synthetically, philosophy analytically

Any general concept can be arrived at in two ways: either through *arbitrary connection of concepts* or by *separation* from that knowledge which is clarified by analysis. Mathematics never forms definitions except in the first way. Consider arbitrarily, for example, four straight lines which enclose a plane surface so that the opposite sides are not parallel. This figure is called a trapezium. The concept which I am explaining is not given before the definition. A cone may signify elsewhere what it will; in mathematics it originates from the arbitrary representation of a right-angled triangle rotated on one of its sides. The explanation obviously originates here, and in all other cases, through *synthesis*.

In the case of definitions of philosophy the situation is quite different. Here the concept of a thing is already given, but it is confused or insufficiently determined. I have to analyse it; I have to compare the separated characteristics together with the given concept in all kinds of cases; I have to develop these abstract thoughts in detail and render them determinate. Everyone, for example, has a concept of time. This concept should be clarified. I have to examine this idea II 277 in all kinds of connection in order to discover its qualities by analyses; I have to combine different abstracted characteristics to see whether they produce a satisfactory concept; I have to collate them together to see whether one does not

6

partly include the other in itself. If I had wished to try to arrive at a definition of time synthetically, what a fortunate accident would have had to occur if this concept were exactly that which our given idea expressed to perfection!

However, it will be said: philosophers sometimes give synthetic explanations as well, and mathematicians analytic ones. For example, when the philosopher arbitrarily conceives a substance with the faculty of reason and calls it a mind. My reply is: such determinations of the meaning of a word are never philosophical definitions; on the contrary, even if they are to be called explanations, they are only grammatical. For philosophy is in no way required to say what name I wish to attach to an arbitrary concept. *Leibniz* conceived a simple substance that had nothing other than obscure representations; he called it a *slumbering monad*; he simply thought it. For its concept was not given to him but rather created by him. Mathematicians have, on the other hand, sometimes given analytic explanations, I admit; but it has always been an error as well. It was in this way that *Wolff* considered similarity in geometry with the eye of a philosopher, intending to subsume the geometrical concept of similarity under the general notion of similarity. He could, however, have well abandoned the task; for when I think of geometrical figures in which the angles included by the lines of the outline are reciprocally equal, and the sides which they include have one and the same relation, then this can always be regarded as the definition of the similarity of geometrical figures; and similarly with the remaining spatial similarities. The general definition of similarity is of no consequence whatever to the geometer. It is fortunate for mathematics that, even though the geometer engages from time to time in such analytical explanations as a result of a false idea of his task, in the end nothing is actually deduced by him, or, if so, his most immediate inferences constitute, basically, the mathematical definition. Otherwise this branch of knowledge would be liable to exactly the same unfortunate discord as philosophy itself.

The mathematician is often concerned with concepts which are capable of a philosophical explanation, as well as a mathematical one, for example, the concept of space in general. But he accepts such a concept as *given* in accordance with his clear and ordinary representation. Sometimes philosophical explanations are given to him from other branches of knowledge, especially in applied mathematics, for example, the explanation of fluidity. But such a definition does not originate within mathematics itself; it is only employed there. It is the business of philosophy to analyse concepts which are given confusedly, to explain them in detail and to make them determinate. The business of mathematics, however, is to combine and to compare the given concepts of magnitudes, which are clear and certain, in order to see what can be deduced from them.

II 278

§2

Mathematics in its reductions, proofs and conclusions examines the universal under symbols in concreto; *philosophy examines the universal by means of symbols* in abstracto

Since we are here treating our propositions as immediate conclusions from experience, I appeal first of all, with regard to the present matter, to arithmetic, both the general arithmetic of indeterminate magnitudes, as well as that of numbers, where the relation of magnitude to unity is determinate. In both kinds of arithmetic symbols are first of all supposed, instead of the things themselves, together with the special notations of their increase or decrease and their relations etc. Afterwards, one proceeds with these signs, according to easy and certain rules, by means of substitution, combination, or subtraction and many kinds of transformations, so that the things symbolised are here completely ignored, until, at the end, in the conclusion the meaning of the symbolical conclusion is interpreted. *Secondly*, in geometry, in order to discover the properties of all circles, a circle is drawn; then, instead of drawing all the possible lines that intersect inside the circle, two lines only are drawn. From these two lines the relations are proved, and in them is observed, *in concreto*, the universal rule of the relations of intersecting lines inside any circle.

If one compares the procedure of philosophy with this, it becomes evident that it is entirely different. The signs used in the philosophical way of thinking are never anything other than words, which can neither show, in their composition, the parts of the concepts out of which the whole idea, indicated by the word, consists; nor can they show in II 279 their combinations the relations of philosophical thoughts. Thus, in all reflection, in this kind of knowledge, one must have the matter itself before one's eyes and one is obliged to conceive the universal abstractly, without being able to avail oneself of that important facility: namely handling the individual symbols themselves, instead of the universal concepts of things. If the geometer, for example, wishes to demonstrate that space is infinitely divisible, he takes, say, a straight line, standing vertically between two parallel lines, and projects other lines from a point on one of these parallel lines, which intersect such lines. He recognises, with the greatest certainty, from this symbol, that this division must go on endlessly. On the other hand, when the philosopher wishes to demonstrate, say, that every body consists of simple substances, he will first of all assure himself that a body is really a whole composed of substances, and that, as far as they are concerned, the composition is an accidental state, without which they could well exist; that, consequently, all composition in a body could be suspended in imagination, so that the substances, out of which the body is composed, still exist and, since that which remains from a compound, when all composition in general is suspended, is simple, bodies must consist of simple substances. Here neither figures nor visible signs can express either the thoughts or their relations; nor can the transposition of symbols, according to rules, be substituted for abstract observation, so that the representation of the matters them-

9

selves is exchanged, in this procedure, for the clearer and easier representation of signs. Rather must the universal be considered in abstraction.

§3

In mathematics there are only a few unanalysable concepts and unprovable propositions; but in philosophy they are innumerable

The concept of magnitude in general, of unity, of quantity, of space, etc., are at least in mathematics unanalysable; their analysis, namely, and explanation does not belong to this branch of knowledge at all. I am well aware of the fact that many geometers confuse the limits of the different branches of learning, and sometimes wish to philosophise in the science of magnitude. Thus, they seek to explain such concepts too, even though the definition has no mathematical consequences at all, in such a case. But this much is certain: any concept is unanalysable with respect to a given discipline if, whether clarifiable or not elsewhere, it does not require to be analysed in this branch of learning. And I have said that such concepts are rare in mathematics. I will go further still and assert: that really no such concepts can occur in mathematics, meaning that their clarification by conceptual analysis does not belong to mathematical knowledge—even assuming that it were possible elsewhere. For mathematics never clarifies a given concept by analysis, but an object is explained by means of arbitrary combination, whose thought first becomes possible in just this way.

When one compares philosophy with this, what a difference is to be seen. In all its disciplines and especially in metaphysics, each and every analysis that can occur is actually necessary; for both the clearness of the knowledge, as well as the possibility of trustworthy deductions, is dependent on this analysis. But it can be seen immediately in advance that it is unavoidable that, in the analysis, unanalysable concepts will be reached: unanalysable either in and for themselves or relatively to us. It is also clear that

there will be uncommonly many such unanalysable concepts, since it is impossible that universal knowledge of such
great complexity should be compounded from a few basic
concepts. Hence it is that many concepts can scarcely be
analysed at all, for example, the concept of a *representation*,
the concept of *being next to* or *after one another*; other concepts
can be only partially analysed, as the concept of *space*, *time*,
of the various *feelings* of the human soul, of the feeling of the
sublime, of the *beautiful*, of the *disgusting*, etc. Without an
exact knowledge and analysis of these concepts the springs
of our nature are not sufficiently known; and, at the same
time, someone who carefully attends to these things will
perceive that the analysis will be far from adequate. I
admit, the explanations of *desire* and *aversion*, of *appetite* and
abhorrence and of innumerable similar concepts are never
given through sufficient analyses. But I am not surprised by
this unanalysability. For with concepts of such various
natures, diverse basic concepts must, in all likelihood, form
their foundation. The mistake, that some have committed,
of treating all such departments of knowledge like those
which can be reduced to a few simple concepts, is similar
to the mistake into which the early physicists fell—that all
the matter of nature consists of the so-called four elements,
a view discredited by better observation.

Further, there are only a few fundamental unprovable II 281
propositions in mathematics, which, even if capable of proof
elsewhere, are regarded as immediately certain in this
branch of knowledge. For example: *The whole is equal to all
the parts taken together; there can only be one straight line between
two points.* Mathematicians are accustomed to set up such
basic propositions at the beginning of their disciplines, so
that it is clear that no other propositions are assumed as
true, except such evident propositions. Everything else,
however, is strictly proved.

When philosophy, and metaphysics in particular, is compared with this, I would, indeed, like to see drawn up a
table of the unprovable propositions, lying at the basis of

this department of knowledge, throughout its whole extent. This would certainly constitute a project that would be immeasurable; but the seeking out of these unprovable, basic propositions is the most important business of higher philosophy. These discoveries will never reach an end, so long as such knowledge as this continues to extend itself. Whatever the object may be, those characteristics, which the understanding initially and immediately perceives in it, are the data for just so many unprovable propositions, which constitute the foundation from which definitions can be drawn up. Before I set about explaining what space is, I clearly perceive that, since this concept is given to me, I must first of all seek out, by analysis, those characteristics which are initially and immediately thought in it. I notice, accordingly, that there are many things external to each other; that this multiplicity of things is not substances, for I do not wish to know what *things* in space are, but rather what *space* itself is; that space can only have three dimensions etc. It is probably possible to explain such propositions, insofar as one examines them *in concreto*, in order to understand them intuitively; but they never permit of proof. For on what basis could this come to pass? for these propositions constitute the first and simplest thoughts, which I am able to entertain of my object, when I begin reflecting on it. In mathematics the definitions are the first thought which I can have of the thing explained. The reason is that my concept of the object takes its origin, in the first place, from the explanation. It is, therefore, simply confused to regard it as provable. In philosophy, where the concept of the thing to be explained is given, that which is immediately and first of all perceived in it, must serve as an
II 282 unprovable basic judgement. Since I do not yet possess the complete and clear concept of the thing, but am just beginning to look for it, it cannot be proved from this concept at all; much rather, it serves to produce, by that means, this clear knowledge and a definition. Before any philosophical explanation of things I must have certain primary funda-

mental judgements. The only mistake that can be committed here is to regard that as an original primary characteristic, which is merely a derived characteristic. In the following reflection, certain things will be mentioned which will place this beyond doubt.

§4

The object of mathematics is easy and simple; that of philosophy however is difficult and involved

Since magnitude constitutes the object of mathematics, and since, in the consideration of this, one only examines how many times something is posited, it becomes clear that this knowledge must rest on a few, very basic doctrines of the general theory of magnitudes, which is really general arithmetic. The increase and decrease of magnitudes, their reduction to equal factors, by the doctrine of roots, is also there seen to originate from a few simple basic concepts. A few fundamental concepts of space effect the application of this general knowledge of magnitudes to geometry. In order to convince oneself one may, for example, compare merely the easy intelligibility of an arithmetical object, which includes within itself an enormous complexity, with the much more difficult intelligibility of a philosophic idea, in which one seeks to know only a little. The relation of a *trillion* to unity is quite clearly understood, whereas philosophers have so far not been able to make intelligible the concept of *freedom* from its elements, that is, from its simple and known concepts. That is: there are infinitely many qualities which constitute the proper object of philosophy and their distinction demands an exceedingly great deal. Similarly, it is far more difficult to resolve involved knowledge, by means of analysis, than to combine given, simple bits of knowledge, by means of synthesis, and thus to arrive at conclusions. I know, there are many people who find philosophy very easy in comparison with higher mathematics. But they call everything philosophy which is to be found in

II 283 books bearing that title. The difference is revealed by success. Philosophical knowledge has frequently the fate of opinions and is like the meteors, whose blaze is no promise of their permanence. They disappear, but mathematics remains. Metaphysics is without doubt the most difficult of all human enquiries; but one has never yet been written. The exercise set by the Academy indicates that there is cause to inform oneself about the path along which one intends seeking it in the first place.

SECOND REFLECTION

The only method of achieving the highest possible certainty in metaphysics

Metaphysics is nothing other than a philosophy of the first principles of our knowledge. Accordingly, what had been demonstrated about mathematical knowledge in comparison with philosophy, in the previous reflection, will also be valid with respect to metaphysics. We have seen the considerable and essential differences that are to be met with between the knowledge in both branches of learning. In this connection, one can say with Bishop *Warburton*[1] that nothing has been more damaging to philosophy than mathematics, in particular the imitating its method of thought, in contexts where it cannot possibly be used; though as far as its application in those spheres of philosophy involving knowledge of magnitudes is concerned the situation is quite different; for there its usefulness is immeasurable.

In mathematics I begin by explaining my object, for example, a triangle, a circle, etc.; in metaphysics I may never begin by explaining my object. Far from its being the case that here the definition is the first thing which I know of the object; much rather does it nearly always come last. In mathematics, namely, I have no concept at all of my object until it is given by the definition. In metaphysics I

14

have a concept given to me already, although it is a confused one. My duty is to search for the clear, detailed and determinate formulation of this confused concept. How then can I begin with this confused datum? *Augustine* said:[2] I know well what time is; but if someone asked me, I do not II 284 know. Much activity of developing obscure ideas, of comparing, of subordinating and of limiting must take place here; and I venture to say that, although a great deal that is true and acute has been said about time, yet the real explanation of this notion has never been given. For as far as the explanation of the name is concerned: this is of little or no help to us. For the word is sufficiently well understood for us not to be mistaken about it, without a verbal definition. If one possessed as many concrete definitions as occur in books under this name, with what certainty could one make inferences and draw conclusions from them! But experience teaches the opposite.

In philosophy, and especially in metaphysics, one can often know a great deal about an object with clearness and certainty, and also derive certain conclusions therefrom, before possessing a definition of that same object, even, indeed, when one had no intention at all of producing a definition. I can be immediately certain about various different predicates of any particular thing, in spite of the fact that I do not know enough about that thing to give a detailed and determinate *concept of the thing*, that is a definition. Even if I should never explain what an *appetite* is, nevertheless I could still say with certainty that every appetite presupposes a representation of the object of the appetite; that this representation is an expectation of the future; that the feeling of desire is bound up with that of appetite, etc. Everyone constantly perceives this in the immediate consciousness of appetite. A definition of appetite could indeed perhaps be reached from the collation of such remarks as those just made. But as long as it is possible to infer what is being sought from a few immediately certain characteristics of that thing without a definition, it is unnecessary to attempt an undertaking of so precarious a nature. In mathematics, as is well known, it is quite different.

In mathematics the meaning of the signs is certain, for it is easy to become conscious of the meaning one wished to attribute to the signs. In philosophy generally and metaphysics in particular, words have their meaning through common usage, except insofar as the meaning of the words is more precisely determined by logical limitation. But the same words are often used of concepts which are very similar but which, however, contain concealed yet considerable differences. Hence, even though the denomination of these concepts seems to be exactly confirmed by common usage, one must here make sure, most carefully, at every use of the concept, whether it really is one and the same concept that is connected with the same sign. We say: someone *distinguishes* gold from brass when he knows, for example, that the density which occurs in the one metal is not to be found in the other. It is also said: an animal *distinguishes* one kind of provender from another when it eats the one and leaves the other. Here, the word 'distinguishes' is used in both cases. But in the first case it means something like: to know *the difference* and this cannot ever occur without *making a judgement*. In the second case, however, it merely indicates that, by different representations, *different actions are performed*: here it is not necessary that a judgement should occur. In the case of the animal we only perceive that it is impelled to different actions through different sensations. This may well be possible, without the animal having to judge in the least about agreement or difference.

The rules of the method, according to which the highest possible metaphysical certainty can alone be achieved, flow quite naturally from all this. They are quite different from the rules which until now have been followed. They promise, where they are applied, as happy a conclusion as could never have been expected along a different path. The *primary* and pre-eminent *rule* is this: that one ought not to

II 285

start with explanations, except, may be, where a dictionary definition only is to be sought, for example, that of which the opposite is impossible is necessary. But even here, there are only a few cases where a clear and definite concept can be confidently established right at the beginning. One ought, on the contrary, to start looking carefully for what is immediately certain in the object, even before a definition has been reached. From this are drawn conclusions. One aims chiefly at deriving true and entirely certain judgements about the object, without making a show of a hoped for explanation. This is never attempted except when it offers itself clearly from the most evident judgements. The second rule is this: that one ought particularly to distinguish the immediate judgements about the object, from that which one meets first of all in it with certainty. After one is certain that the one is not contained in the other, one advances them as the foundation of all inferences, like the axioms of geometry. From this it follows that in metaphysical reflec- II 286 tions one should always particularly distinguish what is certainly known, even if it is little. One can, however, experiment with what is not known for certain, in order to see whether it may not put us on the scent of certain knowledge. But this may only so be done that one does not confuse it with the former. I will not introduce the other procedural rules, which are common to this and every other rational method. I shall only proceed to clarify these rules by means of examples.

The true method of metaphysics is basically the same as that introduced by *Newton* into natural science and which had such useful consequences in that field. It is said there that the rules, according to which certain natural phenomena occur, should be sought by means of certain experience and, if need be, with the help of geometry. Although the first principle is not perceived in the bodies, nevertheless it is certain that they operate according to this law. Involved natural occurrences are explained, when it is clearly shown how they are contained under these well

proved rules. It is exactly the same in metaphysics: by
means of certain inner experience, that is by means of an
immediate evident consciousness, you ought to seek out
those characteristics which certainly lie in the concept of
any general condition; and, even though you do not know
immediately the whole essence of the thing, yet you can
still safely make use of it, in order to derive a great deal
about the thing.

Example

illustrating the only certain method
of metaphysics from knowledge of the
nature of bodies

For the sake of brevity, I refer to a proof which is briefly
indicated at the end of the second paragraph of the first
reflection, in order first of all to lay down the fundamental
proposition that every body consists of simple substances.
Without going into the question what a body is, I know
with certainty that it consists of parts which would exist
even if they were not connected together. And if the concept
of a substance is an abstract concept, so doubtless is the
concept of physical things in the world. However, it is not
even necessary to call them substances. It is sufficient that
it is possible to make inferences from this with the greatest
certainty, that a body consists of simple parts. The certain
II 287 analysis of this is easy, but too lengthy here. Now, I can
demonstrate by means of infallible geometrical proofs that
space does not consist of simple parts. The arguments for
this are sufficiently well known. According to this argument, there is a determinate number of parts to each body
and they are all simple; there is a like number of spatial
parts, taken up by the parts of the body; and they are all
compounded. From this it follows that each simple part
(element) in the body takes up some space. If I now ask:
what does it mean, to take up space? I shall realise, without
bothering about the essence of space, that if space can be

penetrated by anything, without there being anything there resisting, one may well say, if one is inclined, that there could be something in this space, but never, that this space is taken up with something. I recognise from this, that a space is taken up with something, when something is there which resists a moved body trying to penetrate that space. This resistance, however, is impenetrability. Accordingly, bodies take up space by impenetrability. But, impenetrability is a *force*, for it gives expression to a resistance, that is, an action opposed to an external force. And the force which belongs to a body, must belong to its simple parts. Consequently, the elements of every body fill their space by the force of impenetrability. I ask further, however: are not primary elements then extended for that very reason, since everything in the body fills a space? For once, I can here introduce an immediately certain explanation, namely: that that is extended which, posited in itself (absolutely), fills a space, in the same way that every individual body would take up a space, even if, at the same time, I imagine that nothing else existed apart from it. But when I reflect upon a merely simple element, assuming that it is posited by itself, without being connected with other things, it is impossible that there should exist within it a multiplicity of things, external to each other, and that it should occupy a space absolutely. Therefore it cannot be extended. But, since the reason why the element occupies a space, is its power of impenetrability directed against many external things, I see that out of it flows a multiplicity in its external action, but no multiplicity with regard to its internal parts; and consequently the element is not extended because it occupies space in the body (in connection with other elements—*in nexu cum aliis*).

I shall say a little more to make it evident how superficial the proofs of metaphysicians are when, according to custom, they confidently draw inferences from the explanation, once laid down as a foundation—inferences that are immediately lost, if the definition is deceptive. It is well

II 288

known that the majority of *Newtonians*[3] go still further than *Newton* himself and assert that bodies attract each other immediately at a distance (or, as they express it, through empty space). I will not dispute the correctness of this proposition, which certainly has much to be said for it. But I assert that metaphysics has, at least, not refuted it. First of all, bodies are *at a distance* from one another when they do *not touch*. This is precisely the meaning of the word. I now ask: what do I understand by touch? Without bothering about a definition, I become aware of judging that I indeed touch a body from the resistance of its impenetrability. For I find that this concept originally springs from the feeling, in the same way as I also suppose from the judgement of the eye, that one piece of matter will touch another; but I only know it for certain when I first notice the resistance of impenetrability. In this way, when I say: one body has an immediate effect on another at a distance, this means: the one body has an immediate effect on the other, but not by means of impenetrability. But from this it cannot at all be seen why this should be impossible, for someone must demonstrate that impenetrability is either the only force of a body, or, at least, that it cannot have an effect on another body, without at the same time doing so by the agency of impenetrability. But since this has never been proved and, as far as appearances go, would be proved only with difficulty, metaphysics has no good reason at all to rebel against immediate attraction at a distance. However, let the arguments of the metaphysicians make their appearance. First and foremost appears the definition: the immediate, reciprocal presence of two bodies is contact. From this it follows: when two bodies immediately affect each other, then they touch each other. Things that touch each other are not distant from each other. Consequently two bodies never affect each other immediately at a distance, etc. The definition is surreptitious. Not every immediate presence is a contact, but only that by means of impenetrability. All the rest is without foundation.

I proceed further with my treatise. It becomes clear from the example given, that a great deal can be said with certitude about an object, both in metaphysics, as well as in other branches of knowledge, without the object being explained. For here, it has not been explained what body is, nor what space is, and yet one is in possession of reliable propositions about both. What I am trying to say is primarily this: in metaphysics one must proceed entirely by analysis. For the business of metaphysics is indeed the disentangling of confused knowledge. If one compares this with the procedure of philosophers, in vogue in all schools, how mistaken it will be found! The most abstract concepts, to which the understanding naturally proceeds last of all, constitute with them the starting point. The reason is that they have firmly fixed in their heads the mathematician's plan, which they wish completely to imitate. Thus is to be found a curious difference between metaphysics and every other science. In geometry and the other sciences of the theory of magnitudes, one begins with what is easier and advances to the more difficult exercises. In metaphysics, the beginning is constituted by what is most difficult: possibility and existence in general, necessity and contingency, etc.—nothing but concepts of great abstraction and requiring great attentiveness, particularly since their symbols suffer many imperceptible corruptions in use and attention must be paid to these differences. One is supposed to proceed entirely synthetically. Thus, one gives explanations right at the beginning and blithely makes inferences from them. Philosophers congratulate each other, in this vein, for having learned from the geometers the secret of thorough thinking, without at all noticing that geometers acquire concepts by means of *synthesis*, while philosophers can only do so by means of *analysis*. This completely alters the method of thought.

On the other hand, as soon as philosophers enter the natural path of healthy reason and begin by looking for what they know with certainty of the abstract concept of an object (for example space or time) without making any claim to explain anything; if they make inferences from these certain data; if they take note of every changed application of a concept, to see whether the concept itself here remains unchanged, irrespective of whether the symbol of the concept is the same;—if they do this they will perhaps have fewer views to offer; but those which they do put forward will be of certain value. Of the latter I wish to II 290 adduce one example more. Most philosophers advance, as an example of obscure concepts, those which we may have in deep sleep. *Obscure* representations are those of which one is not conscious. Now some experiences indicate that we do have representations in deep sleep, and since we are not conscious of them, they are consequently obscure. Here *consciousness* has a double significance. One is either not conscious that one is having a representation, or one is not conscious that one has had a representation. The former indicates the obscurity of the representation, as it is in the soul; the second indicates nothing more than that one no longer remembers it. The example adduced simply makes clear that there can be representations of which one has no remembrance, when one is awake. But it by no means follows from this that they were not conscious and clear in sleep; as in the example of Herr *Sauvage*[4] of the catalyptic or with the ordinary actions of sleep walkers. However, in this case a great secret of nature has, in all probability, escaped note, due to the fact that one starts drawing conclusions all too readily, without always having first given significance to the concept, by attending to different cases—the secret being namely: that it is, perhaps, in the deepest sleep that the greatest readiness of soul in rational thought may be exercised. For there is no argument to the contrary, apart from the fact that one does not have any memory of it, when one is awake. But this argument proves nothing.

It is far from being the time for proceeding synthetically in metaphysics. Only when analysis has helped us towards clearly and fully understood concepts, will it be possible for

22

synthesis to subordinate compound knowledge to the simplest knowledge, as in mathematics.

THIRD REFLECTION

Of the nature of philosophical certainty

§1

Philosophical certainty is of an entirely different nature from mathematical certainty

Insofar as one knows that it is impossible that a piece of knowledge should be false, it is certain. Taken objectively, the degree of this certainty depends on the sufficiency in the characteristics of the necessity of a truth; but, insofar as it is II 291 regarded subjectively, the certainty is greater, in proportion as the knowledge of this necessity is more intuitive. Mathematical certainty is of a different kind from the philosophical, in both respects. I shall demonstrate this as clearly as possible.

Like every other force of nature, human understanding is bound by certain rules. A mistake is made, not because the understanding joins concepts together without rule, but because a characteristic is denied of a thing, that characteristic not having been perceived in the thing: one judges that, that of which one is *not conscious* in a thing, *does not exist.* Now *firstly*, mathematics reaches its concepts synthetically and is able to assert that, what it did not wish to represent in its object, by the definition, is not contained in it, either. For the concept of what is explained takes its origin, in the first instance, from the explanation, and has no further significance at all, apart from that given it, by the definition. Compared with this, philosophy and metaphysics, in particular, is far more uncertain in its explanations, if it wishes to venture them. For the concept of what has to be explained is given. If one or other of its characteristics escapes notice, which notwithstanding belongs to its complete discrimination; and if it is supposed that no such necessary characteristic is lacking to the full concept, the definition is false and deceptive. We could produce innumerable examples of such a mistake; but I limit myself to the example of contact only, adduced above. *Secondly*, mathematics, in its inferences and proofs, examines its universal knowledge concretely, under signs; but philosophy always examines its universal knowledge, *in abstracto*, alongside the signs. This constitutes a notable difference in the way each arrives at certainty. For since mathematical signs are sensuous epistemological tools, it is possible to know that no concept has been neglected and that each single comparison has occurred, according to easy rules, etc.—it is possible to know this with the same confidence with which one is assured of what one sees with one's eyes. The attention is thereby considerably relieved, for it does not have to consider things in their universal representation, but only the signs known individually and sensibly. Words, as the signs of philosophical knowledge, on the other hand, only help one to remember the universal concepts designated. At all times, their meaning must be held before one's eyes and the pure understanding maintained in constant effort; and how imperceptibly does a characteristic of an abstracted concept escape us, for there is nothing sensible to reveal its omission to us. And then again, different things are held to be the same, and mistaken knowledge is born.

II 292

It has now been demonstrated here, that the arguments from which the conclusion can be drawn: that to have been mistaken in a certain piece of philosophical knowledge is impossible, are never, in themselves, similar to those with which one is faced in mathematics. But apart from this, the intuitive nature of the knowledge—as far as the correctness is concerned—is greater in mathematics than in philosophy; for in the former the object is regarded concretely, in sensible signs; but, in the latter, the object is always examined only in universal, abstract concepts, whose clear impression can-

24

not be nearly so great as that of the former. In geometry, where the symbols bear a similarity, moreover, to the things symbolised, the clearness is still greater, although in algebra the certainty is just as reliable.

§2

Metaphysics is capable of a certainty which is sufficient for conviction

Metaphysical certainty is the same as that of any other philosophical knowledge, for the latter can only possess certainty, if it accords with the general principles furnished by the former. It is known from experience that, even outside mathematics, we can in many cases be perfectly certain, to the extent of conviction, by means of rational argument. Metaphysics is only philosophy applied to more general rational judgements. This situation, with regard to metaphysics, could not possibly be different.

Mistakes are not originated merely by not knowing certain things, but by taking it upon oneself to make judgements, although one does not yet know everything requisite for judgement. A great number of falsehoods, indeed, almost the whole totality of them, owe their origin to this latter precipitateness. Some predicates are known with certainty of a thing. Good! Make them the basis of your inferences and you will not go wrong. But you are set on a definition. Nonetheless you are not sure that you know everything requisite to a definition; and since you still venture a definition regardless of this, you fall into error. It is thus possible to avoid errors, if one seeks out certain and clear knowledge, without however pretending so lightly to definitions. Furthermore, you could safely infer a considerable part of a certain consequence. But do not allow yourself to infer the whole series of consequences, even though the difference may appear but slight. I admit that the proof which we have possessed, that the soul is not material, is a good one. But be careful not to infer from this, that the soul is not of

II 293

25

material nature. For people understand by this, not only that the soul is not material, but also that it is not a simple substance of the kind which an element of matter could be. This requires a special proof, namely: that this thinking being does not exist like a physical element in space, by means of impenetrability, nor that it could constitute along with others an extended thing or mass. No proof has really been given of this; if it were discovered, it would show the unintelligibility of the supposition that a mind can be present in space.

§3

The certainty of the primary fundamental truths of metaphysics is no different in kind from that of every other rational knowledge, with the exception of mathematics

In our times, the philosophy of Herr *Crusius**[5] tries to give to metaphysical knowledge quite a different form, by refusing to attribute to the Law of Contradiction that prerogative of being the universal and highest principle of all knowledge. He introduced many other immediately certain and unprovable propositions and asserted that their correctness
II 294 would be understood from the nature of our understanding, according to the rule that what I cannot think of as otherwise than true, is true. With such principles are numbered among others: what I cannot think of as existing, has never existed; everything must be somewhere and somewhen; and such like. I will indicate, in a few words, the true character of the primary fundamental truths of metaphysics and at the same time indicate the true concept of Herr *Crusius'*

* I have found it necessary to make mention here of the method of this new philosophy. It has quickly become so famous and has offered a so widely admitted service, by virtue of its better clarification of many views, that it would be an essential lack to pass it over in silence, where metaphysics in general is being discussed. What I here touch upon is simply the method peculiar to it; for the difference in individual propositions is not yet sufficient to indicate an essential difference between one philosophy and another.

method, which is not so far removed from the philosophical mode of thought in this piece, as one may perhaps think. It will also be possible to derive from these considerations the degree of certainty possible in metaphysics, in general.

All true judgements must either be affirmative or negative. Since the *form* of all *affirmation* is this: that something is represented as a characteristic of a thing, that is, as one with the characteristic of a thing; every affirmative judgement is thus true, if the predicate is *identical* with the subject. Since the *form* of every *negation* consists in this: that something is represented as contradicting a thing; every negative judgement is thus true, if the predicate *contradicts* the subject. The proposition, therefore, which expresses the essence of every affirmation, and at the same time contains the highest formula of all affirmative judgements runs: a predicate belongs to any subject, when the predicate is identical with the subject. This is the *Law of Identity*. And since the proposition which expresses the essence of all negation: a predicate does not belong to any subject, where the predicate contradicts the subject, is the *Law of Contradiction*, is the first formula of all negative judgements, both together constitute the highest and universal principles of the whole of human reason in the formal understanding. It is here that the majority of people have gone wrong, in having attributed to the Law of Contradiction that rank, with respect to all truths, which it really only has with regard to negative truths. But each proposition that is thought immediately under one of these highest principles and not thinkable in any other way, is unprovable; namely, when either the identity or the contradiction lies immediately in the concepts and cannot, or may not, be apprehended through analysis, by means of an intermediary characteristic. All other propositions are provable. That a body is divisible, is a provable proposition, for one can show the identity of the predicate and subject by analysis and thus mediately. Body is *compound*; but what is compound is *divisible*; consequently a body is divisible. The mediary characteristic is here *being*

II 295 *compound.* Now in philosophy there are many unprovable propositions, such as were indeed adduced above. These are all subordinate to the formal primary principles, but immediately subordinate. But, insofar as they also contain the foundations of other knowledge, they are the primary material principles of the human understanding. For example, that *a body is compound* is an unprovable proposition, for the predicate can only be thought as an immediate and primary characteristic in the concept of the body. Such material principles constitute, as *Crusius* rightly says, the foundation and firmness of human reason. For, as we mentioned above, they are the stuff of explanations, and the data, from which inferences can be drawn with certainty, even when one has no explanation.

Crusius is right also to criticise other schools of philosophy for ignoring these material principles and concentrating merely on the formal principles. For from these alone nothing can really be proved at all, since propositions containing the mediary concept are required; by their means the logical relations of other concepts ought to be recognisable in a rational inference; and among these propositions some must be the first. But the value of the highest material propositions can never be attributed to a number of propositions, if they are not evident to every human understanding. I hold, however, that various propositions advanced by *Crusius* permit of even considerable doubt.

As far as the highest rule of all certainty is concerned, which this famous man proposed placing at the head of all knowledge, and therefore at the head of metaphysical knowledge too; that *what I cannot think of as other than true, is true,* etc., it is easy to see that this proposition could never be the foundation of the truth of any branch of knowledge. For when one admits that no other foundation for truth can be given, except that one cannot possibly hold it for other than true, one gives to understand that no further basis for truth can be given, and that the knowledge is unprovable. Now there may be, of course, many unprovable pieces of knowledge; but the feeling of conviction with respect to them, although an avowal of their truth, is not an argument for it.

According to this theory metaphysics has no formal or material grounds of certainty different in kind from those of geometry. In both occurs the formula of judgements according to the Laws of Identity and of Contradiction. In both, unprovable propositions constitute the foundation of the inferences. Except that, because definitions in mathematics are the primary unprovable concepts of the thing explained, in metaphysics the various unprovable propositions must be given by the first data, instead of by definitions. But they can be just as certain and they either offer material for explanations or they offer the basis of certain inferences. Metaphysics is as much capable of the certainty necessary for conviction as mathematics is; only the latter is easier and partakes of a greater intuition.

II 296

FOURTH REFLECTION

Of the clearness and certainty of which the fundamental principles of natural divinity and ethics are capable

§1

The fundamental principles of natural divinity are capable of the greatest philosophical clearness

Firstly, the differentiation of a thing from all other things can be made most easily and clearly, when this thing is the only one possible of its kind. The object of natural religion is the unique first cause. Its determinations are such that they cannot easily be confused with those of other things. The greatest conviction, however, is possible where it is absolutely necessary that these and no other predicates belong to a thing. For with accidental determinations it is often difficult to discover the variable conditions of its predicates. Hence it is that the absolutely necessary being is an object, such that as soon as one is once on the right scent of its concept, it appears to promise still more certainty than most other philosophical knowledge. In this part of my task, I can do no other than to draw into consideration the possible philosophical knowledge of God in general. For it would take us too far afield to examine the actually existent doctrines of philosophers on this subject. The main concept, which offers itself to the metaphysician here, is the absolutely necessary existence of a being. In order to arrive at this concept, he could first ask *whether it is possible that* II 297 *absolutely nothing at all should exist.* If he now becomes aware that no *existence* at all is given, *nor any to be thought,* and that no *possibility* occur, he may now examine merely the concept of the existence of what must lie at the foundation of all possibility. Thus thought will extend itself and fix the definite concept of the absolutely necessary being. I shall not go into this scheme in detail, but as soon as the existence of the unique, most perfect, and necessary being is apprehended, the concepts of its remaining determinations become much more precise, because they are always the greatest and most perfect; they become also much more certain because those alone that are necessary are attributable. I have, for example, to determine the concept of divine *omnipresence.* I apprehend easily that that being on which everything else is dependent, since it is itself independent, will, by its presence, indeed, determine the *place* of everything else in the world; but it cannot itself have a place among them, for then it would belong to the world. God is, therefore, not really in a place; he is present to all things in all *places* where *things* are. Similarly I see that, while the succession of things to each other in the world is in his power, he does not thereby determine even one point of time in this series, and consequently, with respect to himself, nothing is past or future. When, therefore, I say that God sees the future in advance, this does not mean that God sees what, *with regard to himself, is future,* but rather that he sees what is future, with regard to certain things in the world, that is, what follows a certain state of the world. From this it can be apprehended that there is no difference at all between knowledge of the future, past or present, with respect to the activity of the divine understanding, but that he apprehends them all, as real things of the universe; and this foreseeing can be imagined much more definitely and much more clearly in God than in a thing, belonging to the totality of the world.

In all parts, therefore, where no analogue of chance is to be met, the metaphysical knowledge of God must be very certain. But judgement about his free actions, about his foresight, about the procedure of his justice and goodness, can only have a certainty in this branch of knowledge through approximation, or one which is moral; for here there is still much that is undeveloped even in the concepts that we have of these determinations in ourselves.

§2

According to their present state the fundamental principles of ethics II 298
are not yet capable of all the clearness required

In order to make this clear, I shall only show how little is known of even the primary concept of *obligation*, and how far removed one must be in practical philosophy from producing the clearness and the certainty of the basic concepts and fundamental principles necessary to evidence. The formula in which all obligation is expressed is: One *ought* to do this or that and leave the other. Now every ought expresses a necessity of the action and is capable of a double meaning. I *ought*, namely, either to do something (as a *means*) when I wish something else (as an *end*); or *I ought to do* and realise something else *immediately* (as an end). The former can be called the necessity of the means (*necessitatem problematicam*); the second may be called the necessity of the end (*necessitatem legalem*). The first kind of necessity indicates no obligation at all, but rather only, as the solution to a problem, the prescription which means I must make use of,

31

if I wish to achieve a certain purpose. He who prescribes to another what actions he must perform or leave unperformed if he wishes to further his own happiness, could perhaps, indeed, conceivably subsume all the doctrines of ethics under it. But they are then no longer obligations; or only in the sense in which it would be an obligation to make two intersecting arcs, if I wished to bisect a straight line into two equal parts; that is, it is not an obligation at all, but only advice for proceeding with dexterity, under the assumption that one wishes to achieve an end. Now, since the use of means has no other necessity, apart from that belonging to the end, all the actions prescribed by ethics, under the condition of certain purposes, are accidental and cannot be called obligations, so long as they are not subordinated to a single end, necessary in itself. I ought, for example, to further the total greatest perfection, or I ought to act in accordance with the will of God; to whichever of these two propositions the whole practical philosophy would be subordinated, that proposition, if it is to be a rule and ground of obligation, must order the action as immediately necessary and not on the condition of a certain purpose. And II 299 here we find that such an immediate, ultimate rule of all obligation must be absolutely unprovable. For it is impossible to apprehend, or to infer, what one ought to do from any examination of a thing or a concept, whatever it may be, when, what is supposed, is not an end and the actions are a means. But it cannot be the latter, for then it would be no formula of obligation, but a formula of problematic skill.

And now I can quickly show that, after much reflection on this matter, I am convinced that the rule: do the most perfect possible by you, is the primary *formal ground* of all obligation *to act*, as also the proposition: do not do that which would hinder the greatest possible perfection realisable through you; in respect of duty it *may not be done*. And just as nothing flowed from the first formal principle of our judgement of the true, where no material first grounds are given, so no particularly definite obligation flows from these two rules of the good, where no unprovable material principles of practical knowledge are bound with them.

Only in our times has it begun to be realised that the faculty of representing what is *true* is *knowledge*; whereas the faculty of perceiving what is *good*, is *feeling*; and that these two may not be confused with each other. Now, just as there are unanalysable concepts of what is true, that is, of what is found in the objects of knowledge examined for their own sake, so is there also an unanalysable feeling of the good (this is never found in a thing absolutely, but always in connection with a feeling being). It is a task of the understanding, insofar as it shows how the concept of the good originates from the more simple feelings of the good, to analyse the compound and confused concept of the good and to clarify it. But, if this is simple at all, then the judgement, this is good, is completely unprovable and is an immediate effect of the consciousness of the feeling of desire, combined with the representation of the object. And since there are quite certainly many simple feelings of the good to be found in us, there are many unanalysable representations of the same kind. Accordingly, if an action is immediately represented as good—without the action containing, in a concealed way, a certain other good, apprehendable in it by analysis, and explaining the perfection of the action—the necessity of this action is an unprovable material principle of obligation. For example, love him who loves you is a ɪɪ 300 practical proposition which is indeed subordinate to the supreme formal and affirmative rule of obligation, but immediately subordinate. For since it cannot be further shown by analysis why an especial perfection should exist in mutual love, this rule is not practically proved; that is, is not proved by appealing to the necessity of another perfect action. Rather is it immediately subsumed under the universal rule of good actions. It is possible that my indicated example does not demonstrate the matter sufficiently

33

clearly or convincingly enough. But the limits of a treatise such as the present one, already perhaps overstepped, do not allow me that completeness, which I would well wish. It is an immediate ugliness in the action which contradicts the will of him from whom our existence and everything good comes. This ugliness is clear, even if attention is not paid to the disadvantages, which could accompany such behaviour as consequences. Hence the proposition: do what is in accordance with the will of God, becomes a material principle of ethics, which, notwithstanding, is formally but immediately subordinate to the already mentioned supreme and universal formula. In practical philosophy one must not so lightly take for unprovable what is provable, any more than in theoretical philosophy. Nevertheless, these principles cannot be dispensed with, which, as postulates, contain the foundations for the remaining practical propositions. *Hutcheson*[6] and others have provided, under the name of moral feeling, a beginning to fine observations.

Although it must be possible, indeed, to achieve the highest degree of philosophical clearness in the first grounds of morality, yet, from what I have said, it can be seen that the supreme, fundamental concepts of obligation must first of all be more surely determined. In this respect, the deficiency of practical philosophy is even greater than that of speculative philosophy; for it has still to be discovered in the first place whether the faculty of knowledge or feeling (the first inner ground of the faculty of appetite) exclusively decides the primary principles of practical philosophy.

II 301   POSTSCRIPT

These are the thoughts which I deliver to the judgement of the Royal Academy of Sciences. I dare to hope that the reasons expressed are of some significance to the required elucidation of the matter. I preferred to leave something to be desired with regard to the care, exactness and elegance of the performance, rather than to prevent myself on that account from delivering these thoughts for examination at the appropriate time; particularly since this deficiency can easily be remedied in the case of a favourable reception.

II

Concerning the ultimate foundation of the differentiation of regions in space

II 377 The illustrious *Leibniz* enriched various departments of knowledge with many genuine insights. But the world waited in vain for him to execute projects far greater still. Whether the reason was that his efforts seemed too incomplete to him,—a reservation peculiar to men of distinction, that has continually deprived learning of many valuable fragments, —or whether it was with *Leibniz*, as *Boerhaave*[1] suspects it was with great chemists: that they often claimed the ability to perform certain undertakings, as if they possessed the ability, whereas, in reality, they possessed only the conviction and trust in their own skill, that once they wished to attempt the performance of an undertaking, they could not but be successful: I do not wish to decide here what the explanation is. At least it looks as if a certain mathematical discipline, which he entitled in advance 'Analysis situs', the loss of which *Buffon*,[2] in considering the natural folding together in seeds[3] lamented, was probably never anything more than a thing of the imagination.[4] I do not know how far the object, which I propose to examine here, is related to that which the great man had in mind. To judge from the meaning of words alone, I am engaged in a philosophic search for the ultimate foundation of the possibility of that, of which *Leibniz* intended to determine the magnitudes mathematically. For the positions of the parts of space, in relation to each other, presuppose the region, according to which they are ordered in such a relation. In the most abstract sense, region does not consist of the relation of one thing in space to the next. That would really be the concept

36

of position. Region really consists rather in the relation of the system of these positions to absolute space. The position of the parts of any extended object, with respect to each other, can be sufficiently recognised from the object itself. The region, however, to which this order of the parts is directed, is related to space outside, but not with reference to its localities, for this would be nothing else than the posi- II 378 tion of just those parts in an external relation; region is related rather to space in general as a unity, of which each extension must be regarded as a part. It is no wonder if the reader finds these concepts still very incomprehensible; but they should become clear in due course. I add, therefore, nothing further, except that my intention in this paper is to see whether, in the intuitive judgements of extension, such as include geometry, a clear proof can be found that *absolute space has its own reality independently of the existence of all matter and that it is itself the ultimate foundation of the possibility of its composition.* Everyone knows how futile the efforts of philosophers have been to place this point once and for all beyond dispute, by means of the most abstract judgements of metaphysics. I know of no attempt to execute this a posteriori (namely, by using other undeniable propositions, themselves lying outside the realm of metaphysics, but able, when applied in particular concrete cases, to offer a touch-stone of their correctness), apart from the treatise of the distinguished *Euler* the Elder[5] in the history of the Royal Acadamy of Sciences in Berlin for the year 1748. It did not, however, quite fulfil its purpose, since it only shows the difficulties of giving a definite significance to the most general laws of motion, when the only concept of space that is accepted is that which is derived from the abstraction from the relation of real things. But it leaves untouched the not less significant difficulties which remain, when the sup-posed laws are applied, when one wishes to represent them according to the concept of absolute space, in a particular concrete case. The proof which I am seeking here is intended to place in the hands, not of engineers, as was the intention of Herr *Euler*, but in the hands of geometers themselves a convincing proof that would enable them to assert, with the clearness customary to them, the reality of their absolute space. For this purpose, I make the following preparation.

Because of its three dimensions, three surfaces can be conceived in physical space. They all intersect each other at right angles. Since we know nothing external to us through the senses, except in so far as it stands in relation to ourselves, it is no wonder that we derive from the relation of these intersecting surfaces to our body the ultimate foundation of generating the concept of regions in space. The surface on which the length of our body stands vertically is called, II 379 with respect to ourselves, horizontal; and this horizontal surface gives occasion for the differentiation of objects which we indicate by *above* and *below*. Two other surfaces can stand vertically on this surface and they can, at the same time, intersect each other at right angles, so that the length of the human body is conceived along the line of the intersection. One of these vertical surfaces divides the body into two externally similar halves and gives the foundation of the distinction between the *right* and the *left* half; the other vertical surface which stands perpendicularly to it, enables us to conceive the *front* and *back* side. In a sheet of writing for example, we distinguish the upper from the lower part of the writing; we notice the difference between the front and the back side; and then we notice the position of the written characters from left to right, or vice versa. Turn the sheet how one will, the parts which are ordered on the surface always have the same position here with respect to each other, and the figure is, in all parts, one and the same. But by this representation, the distinction of regions comes so much into consideration and is so closely connected with the impression made by the visible object that the very same piece of writing becomes unrecognisable, when it is seen with everything turned from the right to the left, which before had the opposite position.

38

Even our judgements on terrestrial regions are subordinated to the concept we have of regions in general, in so far as they are determined, in relation to the sides of our bodies. Whatsoever relations we otherwise recognise in the heavens and on the earth, independently of this fundamental concept, are merely the positions of objects in relation to each other. No matter how well I know the order of the parts of the horizon, I can only determine the regions, in accordance with this knowledge, if I am aware of the direction in which the order runs. The most accurate of heavenly charts, no matter how accurately I have it in mind, would not in the end enable me to know from the known region, for example from the north, on which side of the horizon I should seek the rising sun, if, apart from the position of the stars to each other, the regions were not determined by the position of the sketch in relation to my hands. The same holds true of geographical, indeed of our most ordinary knowledge of the position of places; such knowledge is of no help to us, so long as we are unable to place the so ordered things and the whole system of reciprocally related positions, according to II 380 regions, through the relation to the sides of our bodies. There even exists a very noted characteristic of the products of nature, which can itself now and then give occasion to the distinction of kinds, in the definite region where the order of their parts is reversed, and whereby two creatures can be distinguished, even though, in respect both of size and proportion and even of the situation of the parts relative to each other, they may be in perfect agreement.[6] The hair on the crown of the head of all human beings is directed from the left to the right hand side. All hops wind round their poles from left to right; beans, however, twist in the opposite direction. Almost all snails, with the exception of perhaps three species, coil from the left side to the right, looking down from above, that is from the point of the shell to the mouth. This definite quality is immutably present in exactly the same species, without any relation to the hemisphere where they are to be found, or to the direction of the daily

39

movement of the sun and moon which, with us runs from left to right, but which for those living in the Antipodes runs from right to left. This is because, in the natural generations mentioned, the cause of the convolutions lies in the seeds themselves. On the other hand, where a certain turning can be attributed to the course of the heavenly bodies, as for example the law *Mariotte*[7] claims to have observed in the case of the winds, which readily run through the whole compass from left to right from new moon to full moon, then these circular movements must run in the opposite direction in the other hemisphere, as indeed *Don Ulloa*[8] really thinks he has found confirmed by his observations in the southern ocean.

Since the distinct feeling of the right and the left side is of such great necessity to the judgement of the regions, nature has at the same time attached it to the mechanical structure of the human body. By its means one side, namely the right hand one, has an undoubted superiority in skill, and, perhaps, also in strength, over the left. Hence all the peoples of the earth are right handed (leaving aside individual exceptions which, like that of being cross-eyed, cannot upset the universality of the rule, according to the natural order). One moves one's body more easily from the right to the left than in the opposite direction when one mounts a horse or steps over a pit. Everywhere one writes with the right hand and one does everything with it, for which skill or strength II 381 is required. However, just as the right side seems to have the advantage in mobile power, so the left side has the advantage over the right side in respect of sensitivity, if certain scientists are to be believed—for example *Borelli*[9] and *Bonnet*.[10] The former asserts of the left eye and the latter of the left ear that the sense in them is stronger than that in the identically named organ on the right side. And thus it is that both sides of the human body, irrespective of their great external similarity, are sufficiently distinguished, by means of clear sensation, leaving aside the differing situation of the internal parts and the perceptible beating of the heart, since this muscle in its continual contraction touches, in oblique motion, the left side of the breast with its tip.

We wish, therefore, to show that the complete principle of determining a physical form does not rest merely on the relation and the situation of the parts, with respect to each other, but also on its relation to general absolute space, as conceived by geometers; indeed, in such a way that this relation cannot be immediately perceived, though, perhaps, the physical differences that rest uniquely and alone on this ground can be. When two figures, drawn on a flat surface, are like and similar, they cover each other. But it is often different with physical extension or even with lines and surfaces not lying on a flat surface. They can be perfectly like and similar and yet be in themselves so different that the limits of the one cannot at the same time be the limits of the other. The thread of a screw which goes round its pin from left to right will never fit into a nut where the thread runs from right to left, even though the size of the pin and the number of the screw-turns are the same. A spherical triangle can be perfectly like and similar to another without however covering it. But the most common and the clearest example is to be found in the members of the human body, which are ordered symmetrically with respect to the vertical surface. The right hand is similar to and like the left hand, and merely looking at one of them, at the proportion and the situation of the parts to each other, and at the size of the whole, a complete description of the one must apply, in all respects, to the other.

An object which is completely like and similar to another, although it cannot be included exactly within the same limits, I call its *incongruent counterpart*. In order to demonstrate the possibility of an incongruent counterpart a body is taken which does not consist of two halves arranged symmetrically with reference to a single intersecting surface but rather, for example, a *human hand*. From all points of its surface one extends perpendicular lines to a board placed opposite the object. One extends these lines exactly so far behind the board as the points lie before it. When the end points of these so extended lines are connected, they constitute the surface of a bodily figure, which is the incongruent counterpart of the original object. That is, when the given hand is a right hand, its counterpart is a left hand. The reflection of an object in a mirror rests on exactly the same principles. For the object appears always exactly so far behind the mirror as it stands before its surface. Thus the image of a right hand is always a left hand in the mirror. Should the object itself consist of two incongruent counterparts as, for example, does the human body when it is divided from back to front by means of a vertical intersection, then its image is congruent to it. This can be easily seen when one imagines it turned a half circle. For the counterpart of an object's counterpart is, of necessity, congruent to that object.

So much may be sufficient to understand the possibility of completely like and similar and yet incongruent spaces. We turn now to the philosophical application of these concepts. It is already clear from the everyday example of the two hands that the figure of a body can be completely similar to that of another, and that the size of the extension can be, in both, exactly the same; and that yet, however, an internal difference remains: namely, that the surface that includes the one could not possibly include the other. As the surface limiting the bodily space of the one cannot serve as a limit for the other, twist and turn it how one will, this difference must, therefore, be such as rests on an inner principle. This inner principle of difference cannot, however, be connected with the different way in which the parts of the body are connected with each other. For, as one sees from the given example, everything can be perfectly identical in this respect. Let it be imagined that the first created thing were a human

II 383 hand, then it must necessarily be either a right hand or a left hand. In order to produce the one a different action of the creative cause is necessary from that, by means of which its counterpart could be produced.

42

If one accepts the concept of modern, in particular, German philosophers, that space only consists of the external relations of parts of matter, which exist alongside one another, then all real space would be, in the example used, simply that *which this hand takes up*. However, since there is no difference in the relations of the parts to each other, whether right hand or left, the hand would be completely indeterminate with respect to such a quality, that is, it would fit on either side of the human body. But that is impossible.

From this it is clear that the determinations of space are not consequences of the situations of the parts of matter relative to each other; rather are the latter consequences of the former. It is also clear that in the constitution of bodies differences, and real differences at that, can be found; and these differences are connected purely with *absolute and original space*, for it is only through it that the relation of physical things is possible. It is also clear that since absolute space is not an object of external sensation, but rather a fundamental concept, which makes all these sensations possible in the first place, we can only perceive through the relation to other bodies that which, in the form of a body, purely concerns its relation to pure space.

A reflective reader will therefore regard the concept of space in the way geometers regard it, and also as perceptive philosophers have taken it up into the theory of natural science, as other than a mere entity of reason.[11] Nonetheless, there is no lack of difficulties surrounding the concept when one tries to grasp with the ideas of reason its reality, evident enough to the inner sense. But this difficulty appears everywhere, if one still wishes to philosophise about the first data of our experience. But this difficulty is never so decisive as that which emerges, when the consequences of an accepted concept contradict the clearest experience.

III

ON THE FORM AND PRINCIPLES OF THE SENSIBLE AND INTELLIGIBLE WORLD.

A DISSERTATION
FOR THE PROPER OBTAINMENT OF THE POST
OF ORDINARY PROFESSOR OF LOGIC AND METAPHYSIC
WHICH, ACCORDING TO THE REQUIREMENT OF
THE STATUTES OF THE UNIVERSITY,
WILL BE PUBLICLY DEFENDED
BY

IMMANUEL KANT

THE FUNCTION OF RESPONDENT WILL BE
UNDERTAKEN BY

MARCUS HERTZ,

OF BERLIN, OF JEWISH DESCENT
A STUDENT OF MEDICINE AND PHILOSOPHY,
AGAINST OPPONENTS

GEORG WILHELM SCHREIBER

OF KÖNIGSBERG IN PRUSSIA, STUDENT
IN THE FACULTY OF PHILOSOPHY,

JOHANN AUGUST STEIN,

OF KÖNIGSBERG IN PRUSSIA,
CANDIDATE IN BOTH LAWS

AND

GEORG DANIEL SCHRÖTER

OF ELBING, CANDIDATE IN
SACRED THEOLOGY

IN THE LARGE LECTURE THEATRE
AT THE USUAL MORNING AND AFTERNOON HOURS
ON 21ST OF AUGUST OF THE YEAR 1770.[1]
KÖNIGSBERG
AT THE SHOP OF THE ROYAL COURT
AND UNIVERSITY PRINTING WORKS.

TO THE MOST AUGUST,
SERENE AND MIGHTY
PRINCE AND MASTER,
THE LORD FREDERICK,
KING OF THE PRUSSIANS,
MARGRAVE OF BRANDENBURG,
ARCH-CHAMBERLAIN AND ELECTOR OF
THE HOLY ROMAN EMPIRE
SOVEREIGN DUKE OF SILESIA,
ETC. ETC. ETC.
TO THE MOST CLEMENT FATHER
OF HIS COUNTRY,
TO HIS MOST INDULGENT KING AND MASTER,
THESE FIRST-FRUITS OF THE OFFICE
ENTRUSTED TO HIM
ARE OFFERED IN DEVOTION
BY HIS MOST HUMBLE

IMMANUEL KANT

On the notion of a world in general

§1

In a substantial composite, just as analysis does not come to
an end until a part is reached which is not a whole, that is to
say a SIMPLE, so likewise synthesis does not come to an end
until we reach a whole which is not a part, that is to say a
WORLD.

In this exposition of the underlying concept, I have, in
addition to the marks appropriate to a distinct cognition of
the object, also paid some little attention to the *two-fold
genesis* of the concept out of the nature of the mind. For
since this genesis, by serving as an example, can help us to
secure a deeper insight into method in metaphysics, it seems
to me that it should not be underestimated. Thus it is one
thing, given the parts, to conceive for oneself the *composition*
of the whole, by means of an abstract notion of the intellect; and it is another thing to *follow up* this general *notion*,
as one might do with some problem of reason, through the
sensitive faculty of knowledge, that is to represent the same
notion to oneself in the concrete by a distinct intuition. The
former is done by means of the concept of *composition* in general, in so far as a number of things are contained under it (in
mutual relations to each other), and so by means of ideas of
the intellect which are universal. The second case rests upon
temporal *conditions*, in so far as it is possible by the successive
addition of part to part to arrive genetically, that is by
SYNTHESIS, at the concept of a composite, and this case
falls under the laws of *intuition*. In a similar way, when a
substantial composite has been given we arrive without
difficulty at the idea of things which are simple by taking
away generally the intellectual notion of *composition*. For the

things which remain when every element of conjunction has been removed are *simple* things. Under the laws of intuitive cognition, it is true, this does not actually happen, that is to say every element of composition is not taken away, unless we go back from the given whole to all its *possible parts what-*
II 388 *soever*, that is unless we proceed by analysis,* which in its turn rests upon a temporal condition. But for a composite there must be a *manifold* of parts and for a whole there must be an *allness* of parts. So neither the analysis nor the synthesis will be completed, nor will the concept of a *simple* emerge by means of analysis nor the concept of a *whole* by means of synthesis, unless it should be possible to carry out the respective processes in a finite assignable period of time.

But with a *continuous quantity* the *regression* from the whole to the parts that can be given, and with an *infinite* quantity the *progression* from the parts to the given whole, have in each case *no point at which they stop*, and as a result in the one case complete analysis and in the other case complete synthesis would be impossible. So, in accordance with the laws of intuition, in the first case the whole cannot be thought of completely as regards *composition* and in the second case the composite cannot be thought of completely as regards *totality*. From this it is clear how, since *unrepresentable* and *impossible* are commonly treated as having the same meaning, the concepts both of the *continuous* and of the *infinite* come to be rejected by large numbers of people. For indeed, *according to the laws of intuitive cognition*, any representation of these concepts is absolutely impossible. Now although I am

* A double meaning is commonly assigned to the words 'analysis' and 'synthesis'. Thus synthesis is either *qualitative,* a progression within a series of *subordinates* from the ground to the grounded, or *quantitative,* a progression within a series of co-ordinates, from a given part through its complements to the whole. In a similar way analysis, taken in its first sense, is a regression from the *grounded to the ground*, but in its second sense it is a regression from a *whole* to its *possible* or mediate *parts*, that is to say to parts of parts, and so it is not a division but a *subdivision* of a given composite. Here we use both synthesis and analysis only in their second senses.

not here pleading a case for these notions,*—notions which have been expelled in disgrace from a not inconsiderable number of schools, especially the notion of the continuous— none the less it will be of the greatest importance to have given a warning that the people who use such a perverse method of arguing are guilty of the gravest of errors. For whatever is *inconsistent with* the laws of the intellect and of reason is undoubtedly impossible. But anything which as being an object of pure reason simply *does not come under* the laws of intuitive cognition is not in the same position. For this lack of accord between the *sensitive* faculty and the *intellectual* faculty—the nature of these faculties I shall explain later—points only to the fact that *the abstract ideas which the mind entertains when they have been received from the intellect very often cannot be followed up in the concrete and converted into intuitions.* And this *subjective* resistance is, as frequently, no true indication of any *objective* inconsistency, and the incautious

* Those who reject an actual mathematical infinite are not performing a very onerous task. For assuredly they construct their definition of the infinite in such a way as to enable them to carve some contradiction out of it. The *infinite* for them is said to be *that quantity than which a greater quantity is impossible*, and the mathematical infinite is expressed for them as, there is a manifold (of a unit which can be given) than which a larger manifold is impossible. In place of '*infinite*' they then substitute '*largest*' and since a largest manifold is impossible they readily conclude against an infinite which they themselves have constructed. Or else they call an infinite manifold an *infinite number*, and declare that an infinite number is absurd. This last is indeed perfectly obvious but it is a case in which the only fight is with shadows in the structure of our minds. But suppose they conceive of the mathematical infinite as a quantity which when related to a measure treated as a unit constitutes *a manifold larger than any number*, then, if they had further noticed that *measurability* here only denotes relation to the scale of the human intellect, a scale through which it is only possible to reach *the definite concept of a manifold* by the successive addition of one to one and the *complete* concept which is called a *number* only by carrying out this progression in a finite time, they would have seen very clearly that things which do not accord with the law fixed for some one subject do not thereby pass beyond all intellection. For there could be given an intellect, though certainly not a human intellect, which might see a manifold distinctly at a single glance without the successive application of a measure.

are easily deceived by it into taking the limits by which the human mind is circumscribed as limits within which the very essence of things is contained.

Moreover in the case of substantial composites, whether given by the testimony of the senses or in any other way, it can easily be shown by proof based upon grounds of the intellect that both simple things and a world are given. But in framing my definition I have also pointed a finger at the causes for this which lie in the character of a subject, so that the notion of a world may not appear purely arbitrary and, as happens in mathematics, constructed only for the purpose of deducing the consequences which follow from it. For the mind which is intent upon the concept of a composite, whether it be engaged in breaking it up or putting it together, demands and adopts for itself boundaries within which it may find peace from either side, the a priori and the a posteriori.

§2

In the definition of a world the following are the moments which require attention:

I. MATTER (in the transcendental sense), that is the *parts*. These are here taken to be *substances*. I was able to remain wholly unconcerned about the agreement or otherwise of my definition with the ordinary meaning of the word. For the only question here concerns a problem arising under the laws of reason, namely how it is possible for several substances to coalesce into one thing, and upon what conditions it depends that this one thing is not a part of something else. But indeed the force of the word 'world' as it is found in common use springs to the mind of its own accord. For no one assigns *accidents* to a *world* as its parts, but only to its *state* as *determinations*. Hence the so-called world *of the ego*, which is completely constituted by a unique simple substance together with its accidents, is not properly called a world, unless perhaps it is called an *imaginary* world. For the same reason it is wrong to attribute the series of successive things, I mean states, to the world-whole as a part. For modifications are *not parts* of a subject, but are *grounded determinations*. Finally I have not here raised the question of the nature of the substances which constitute the world, namely whether they are *contingent* or necessary. Nor do I II 390 gratuitously store away the determination of this question in my definition, intending subsequently, as often happens, to extract therefrom this very same determination by some fair-seeming method of clever speaking. But I shall later show[2] that the contingency of its substances can be inferred more than sufficiently from the conditions here posited.

II. FORM, which consists in the *co-ordination* of substances, not in their subordination. For *co-ordinates* are related to one another as complements to a whole, while *subordinates* are related to one another as caused and cause, or generally as principle and principled. The first relationship is reciprocal and *homonymous*, so that any correlate is related to the other as determinant and at the same time as determinate. The second relationship is *heteronymous*, being from the one side a relation of dependence only and from the other a relation of causality. This co-ordination is conceived of as *real* and objective, not as ideal and depending upon the mere whim of a subject, whereby you may fashion a whole by making a summation at your pleasure of any manifold whatsoever. For by taking several things together you achieve without difficulty a *whole* of *representation*, but not thereby the *representation of a whole*. Accordingly if there happened to be certain wholes consisting of substances, and these wholes were not bound to one another by any bond, the bringing of these wholes together, whereby the mind forces the manifold into an ideal unity, would not give expression to anything more than a plurality of worlds held together in a single act of thought. But the bond constituting the *essential* form of a world is seen as the principle of the *possible influxes* of the substances which constitute the world. For actual influxes do not pertain to the essence but to the state, and the transeunt forces themselves, which are the causes of the influxes, suppose some principle by which it may be possible that the states of the several things whose subsistence is none the less independent each from the other should be related to one another mutually as grounded determinations. If you depart from this principle you are debarred from positing as possible a transeunt force in the world. And indeed this *form* which is *essential* to a world is for that reason *immutable* and not exposed to any vicissitude. And this is the case in the first place for a *logical reason*. For any change supposes the identity of the subject as the determinations succeed one another. Hence the world, remaining the same world throughout all its successive states, preserves the same fundamental form. For the identity of the *parts* is not sufficient for the identity of the whole, but there is required an identity of characteristic *composition*. But above all the same result follows because of a *real reason*. For the nature of a world, being the first internal principle of each and every one of the variable determinations which pertain to its state, cannot be opposed to itself, and consequently it is by nature immutable, that is it cannot be changed by itself. And so there is given in any world a certain form which must be assigned to its nature, which is constant and II 391 invariable, as the perennial principle of each and every contingent and transitory form pertaining to the state of that world. Those who consider this investigation superfluous are frustrated by the concepts of *space* and *time*. These they treat as conditions already given in themselves and primitive, with whose help, to be sure, and without any other principle, it would be not only possible but also necessary that a number of actual things should be mutually related to one another as component parts and should constitute a whole. But I shall shortly explain that these notions are not *rational* at all, nor are they objective *ideas* of any bond, but they are *phenomena*, and while they do indeed bear witness to some common principle constituting a universal bond, they do not expose it to view.

III. ENTIRETY, which is the *absolute* allness of its component parts. For when we consider some *given* composite, although that composite were still to be a part of another composite, yet there is always present a certain *comparative* allness, namely that of the parts pertaining to that quantity itself. But in this case whatever things are related to one another as component parts with respect to any whole *whatsoever*, those things are taken by the intellect as placed in conjunction. This absolute *totality* may bear on the face of it the appearance of an everyday concept and one that is easily met with, especially when it is stated negatively as happens in a definition. Yet when we reflect upon it more deeply it is seen to constitute a crux for the philosopher. For it is hardly possible to conceive how the *never to be completed series* of the states of the universe which succeed one another to *eternity* can be reduced to a *whole* which comprehends absolutely all its vicissitudes. Indeed it necessarily follows from its very infinity that the series has no *point at which it stops*. And so there is not given any series of things in succession except one which is part of another series. It follows that for this same reason comprehensive completeness or *absolute totality* seems here to have departed altogether. For although the notion of a part could be taken universally and whatever things are contained under this notion might constitute a single thing if they were regarded as placed in the same series, yet it seems to be required by the concept of *a whole* that they should all *be taken simultaneously*. And this in the case given is impossible. For since nothing succeeds the whole series, when we set up a series of things in succession there is nothing given which is not followed by something else except the last of the series. This will be something which is last in eternity and this is absurd. The difficulty which confronts the totality of a successive infinite does not apply, perhaps someone may think, in the case of a *simultaneous infinite*, because *simultaneity* seems expressly to avow a complex *of all things at the same time*. But if a simultaneous infinite were admitted, one must also concede the totality of a successive infinite—for when the latter is denied, the first also is taken away. For a simultaneous infinite provides eternity with unexhausted matter for progressing successively through its innumerable parts to infinity. Yet this II 392 series when completed with all its numbers would be given actually in a simultaneous infinite and so a series which is never to be completed by successive additions nevertheless could be given *as a whole*. Let him who is to extricate himself from this thorny question note that neither the successive nor the simultaneous co-ordination of several things (since both co-ordinations depend on concepts of time) pertains to the *intellectual* concept of a whole, but only to the conditions of *sensitive intuition*. And so even if these co-ordinations were not to be sensitively conceivable, they do not thereby cease to be intellectual. It is sufficient for this concept that co-ordinates should be given, no matter how, and that they should be all thought of as pertaining to one thing.

SECTION II

On the distinction between sensibles and intelligibles in general

§3

Sensuality is the *receptivity* of a subject by which it is possible for the subject's own representative state to be affected in a definite way by the presence of some object. *Intelligence* (rationality) is the *faculty* of a subject by which it has the power to represent things which cannot by their own quality come before the senses of that subject. The object of sensuality is the sensible; that which contains nothing but what is to be cognised through the intelligence is intelligible. In the schools of the ancients the first was called a *phenomenon* and the second a *noumenon*. Cognition in so far as it is subject to the laws of sensuality is *sensitive*, in so far as it

54

is subject to the laws of the intelligence is *intellectual* or rational.

§4

In this way whatever in cognition is sensitive is dependent upon the special character of the subject to the extent that the subject is capable of this or that modification by the presence of objects and these modifications can differ in different cases according to variations in the subjects. But whatever cognition is exempt from such subjective conditions has regard only to the object. Consequently it is clear that things which are thought sensitively are representations of things *as they appear*, but things which are intellectual are representations of things *as they are*. In a representation of sense there is first of all something which you might call the *matter*, namely the *sensation*, and there is also something which can be called the *form*, namely the *specificity* of the sensibles which arises according as the various things which affect the senses are co-ordinated by a certain natural law of the mind. Moreover just as the sensation which consti- II 393 tutes the *matter* of a sensual representation is evidence at least for the presence of something sensible, but in respect of its quality is dependent upon the nature of the subject to the extent that the latter is capable of modification by the object in question, so also the *form* of the same representation is undoubtedly evidence of a certain respect or relation in the sensa. But properly speaking it is not some adumbration or schema of the object, but only a certain law implanted in the mind by which it co-ordinates for itself the sensa which arise from the presence of the object. For objects do not strike the senses in virtue of their form or specificity. So, for the various things in an object which affect the sense to coalesce into some representational whole there is needed an internal principle in the mind by which those various things may be clothed with a certain *specificity* in accordance with stable and innate laws.

§5

So for sensual cognition the matter which is sensation and through which cognitions are called *sensual,* is as pertinent as the form in virtue of which, even if it were to be found quite apart from any sensation, representations are called *sensitive.* In so far as *intellectual* things on the other hand are concerned, it must above all be carefully noted that the use of the intellect or superior faculty of the soul is two-fold. By the first of these uses the concepts themselves, whether of things or relations, *are given* and this is the REAL USE. By the second use no matter what the source from which they are given the concepts are simply *subordinated* to themselves, I mean the lower to the higher (to common marks) and are compared with one another in accordance with the principle of contradiction, and this use is called the LOGICAL USE. Now the logical use of the intellect is common to all the sciences, but the real use is not common to all. For when a cognition has been given no matter how, it is regarded either as contained under a mark common to several cognitions or as opposed to that mark. This can be either immediately and directly as happens in *judgements* leading to a distinct cognition, or mediately as happens in *reasonings* leading to an adequate cognition.[3] So when sensitive cognitions are given, sensitive cognitions are subordinated by the logical use of the intellect to other sensitive cognitions as to common concepts, and phenomena are subordinated to more general laws of phenomena. But it is of the greatest importance here to have noticed that cognitions must always be treated as sensitive cognitions however extensive may have been the operation of the logical use by the intellect upon them. For they are called sensitive *because of their genesis* and not as a result of *comparing* them in respect of identity or opposition. Hence even the most general empirical laws are none the less sensual, and the principles of sensitive form which are found in geometry (relations determined in space), however much the intellect may operate upon them by reasoning

according to the rules of logic from what is given sensitively   II 394
(by a pure intuition), none the less do not pass out of the
class of sensitive things. But in sensual things and in phenomena that which precedes the logical use of the intellect is
called *appearance*, and the reflective cognition which arises
when several appearances are compared by the intellect is
called *experience*. And so there is no passage from appearance
to experience except by reflection in accordance with the
logical use of the intellect. The common concepts of experience are called *empirical*, and the objects of experience
are called *phenomena*, but the laws both of experience and
generally of all sensitive cognition are called laws of phenomena. And so empirical concepts by reduction to a greater
universality do not become intellectual in the *real sense*, and
do not go outside the species of sensitive cognition, but to
whatever point they mount by abstraction, they remain
sensitive indefinitely.

§6

In so far as intellectual things strictly as such are concerned,
where the *use of the intellect* is *real*, such concepts whether of
objects or relations are given by the very nature of the
intellect and they have not been abstracted from any use of
the senses nor do they contain any form of sensitive cognition as such. But it is necessary here to notice the extreme
ambiguity of the word *abstracted*, and I think this ambiguity
must preferably be wiped clean away beforehand lest it
mar our investigation into things intellectual. I mean that
it would be proper to say: *to abstract from some things*, but not:
to abstract something. The first expression indicates that in a
certain concept we should not attend to other things bound
to it no matter how, while the second expression indicates
that it would only be given concretely and in such a way that
it is separated from the things joined to it. Hence an intellectual concept *abstracts* from everything sensitive, but is *not
abstracted* from things which are sensitive, and perhaps it

57

would more rightly be called *abstracting* rather than *abstract*. Accordingly it is more advisable to call intellectual concepts *pure ideas*, and concepts which are only given empirically *abstract* concepts.

§7

From this one can see that the sensitive is badly described as what *is more confusedly* cognised and the intellectual as that of which there is a *distinct* cognition. For these are only logical distinctions and ones which *do not touch* at all the things *given* which underlie every logical comparison. Thus sensitive things can be very distinct and intellectual things
II 395 extremely confused. We notice the first case in the prototype of sensitive cognition, *geometry*, and the second case in the organon of all intellectual things, *metaphysics*. And it is obvious how much effort is devoted by metaphysics to dispelling the clouds of confusion which darken the common intellect, although it is not always so happily successful as geometry is. None the less each and every one of these cognitions preserves the sign of its ancestry, so that the first group, however distinct they be, are called sensitive because of their origin, while the second group, even though confused, remain intellectual, as for example is the case with *moral* concepts which are cognised not by experiencing them but through the pure intellect itself. But I am afraid it may be that the illustrious WOLFF has, by this distinction between things sensitive and things intellectual, which for him is only a logical distinction, completely abolished, to the great detriment of philosophy, that noble institution of antiquity, the discussion of the *character of phenomena and noumena*, and has turned men's minds away from the search into those things to what are very often only logical minutiae.

§8

Now the philosophy which contains the *first principles* of the use of the *pure intellect* is METAPHYSICS. But its propaedeutic science is that science which teaches the distinction of sensitive cognition from intellectual cognition, and it is of this science that I am offering a specimen in my present dissertation. Since, then, empirical principles are not found in metaphysics, the concepts met with in metaphysics are not to be sought in the senses, but in the very nature of the pure intellect, and that not as concepts *born with it*, but as concepts abstracted out of the laws planted in the mind (by attending to its actions on the occasion of an experience), and so as *acquired* concepts. To this genus belong possibility, existence, necessity, substance, cause etc., together with their opposites or correlates. These never enter any sensual representation as parts and so could not be abstracted from it in any way at all.

§9

The use[4] of things intellectual is pre-eminently two-fold. The first is *elenctic*, whereby they are of value negatively, namely when they keep things conceived sensitively away from noumena, and although they do not advance science by the breadth of a fingernail, yet they keep it safe from the contagion of errors. The second is *dogmatic* and in accordance with it the general principles of the pure intellect, such as are displayed in ontology or in rational psychology, issue into some exemplar only to be conceived by the pure intel- II 396 lect and which is a common measure for all other things in so far as they are realities. This exemplar is NOUMENAL PERFECTION. This perfection is what it is either in a theoretic sense* or in a practical sense. In the first sense it is the highest being, GOD, in the second sense it is MORAL PERFECTION. So *moral philosophy*, in as much as it supplies the first *principles of critical judgement*, is only cognised by the pure

* We consider something theoretically to the extent that we attend only to those things which are appropriate to a being, but we consider it practically if we look separately at those things which ought to be present in it.[5]

intellect and itself belongs to pure philosophy. And the man who reduced its criteria to the sense of pleasure or pain, Epicurus, is very rightly blamed, together with certain moderns who have followed him to some extent from afar, such men as Shaftesbury and his supporters. In any genus of things whose quantity is variable it is the *maximum* which is the common measure and principle of cognising. The *maximum* of *perfection* is at the present time called the ideal, while for Plato it was called the idea (as in the case of his idea of the State). It is the principle of all the things which are contained under the general notion of some perfection, in as much as the lesser grades, it is held, can only be determined by limiting the maximum. But God, since as the ideal of perfection he is the principle of cognising, is at the same time, as existing really, the principle of the coming into being of all perfection whatsoever.

§10

There is not given (to man) an *intuition* of things intellectual, but only a *symbolic cognition*, and intellection is only allowable for us through universal concepts in the abstract and not through a singular concept in the concrete. For all our intuition is bound to a certain principle of form under which form alone can something be *discerned* by the mind immediately or as *singular*, and not merely conceived discursively through general concepts. But this formal principle of our intuition (namely space and time) is the condition under which something can be the object of our senses, and so, as the condition of sensitive cognition, it is not a means to intellectual intuition. Moreover while it is only by the senses that all the matter of our cognition is given, the noumenon as such is not to be conceived by means of representations drawn from sensations. So the concept of the intelligible as such has been forsaken by all *things given* in human intuition. Indeed the *intuition* of our II 397 mind is always *passive*. And so it is only possible to the extent that something can affect our senses. But divine intuition, which is the principle of objects and not something principled, since it is independent, is an archetype and for that reason perfectly intellectual.

§11

Now although phenomena are properly species of things and are not ideas, nor do they express the internal and absolute quality of objects, none the less cognition of them is most veridical. For first of all, in as much as they are sensual concepts or apprehensions, they are witnesses, as being things caused, to the presence of an object, and this is opposed to idealism. Then consider judgements about things cognised sensitively. Truth in judging consists in the agreement of a predicate with a given subject. But the concept of a subject, in as much as it is a phenomenon, would only be given[6] through its relation to the sensitive faculty of cognising, and it is in accordance with the same relation that predicates would be given which were sensitively observable. Accordingly it is clear that representations of a subject and a predicate arise according to common laws, and so provide a handle for a most veridical cognition.

§12

Whatever things are referred to our senses as objects are phenomena. But things which, since they do not touch the senses, contain only the singular form of sensuality pertain to pure intuition (that is an intuition which is empty of sensations, but for that reason not intellectual). Phenomena are reviewed and set out, *first* those of external sense, in PHYSICS, *then* those of internal sense, in empirical PSYCHOLOGY. But pure (human) intuition is not a universal or logical concept *under which*, but is a singular concept *in which*, sensibles no matter what are thought, and so it contains the concepts of space and time. These concepts, since in the case of things sensible they determine nothing as to their *quality*, are not objects of science except in respect of *quantity*. Hence PURE MATHEMATICS deals with *space* in GEOMETRY, and *time* in pure MECHANICS. In addition to these concepts there is a certain concept which in itself indeed is intellectual, but whose actuation in the concrete requires the assisting notions of time and space (by successively adding a number of things and setting them simultaneously beside one another). This is the concept of *number*, which is the concept treated in ARITHMETIC. So pure mathematics, giving expression to the form of all our

II 398 sensitive cognition, is the organon of each and every intuitive and distinct cognition. And since its objects themselves are not only the formal principles of every intuition, but are themselves *original intuitions*, it provides us with the most veridical cognition and at the same time an exemplar of the highest kind of evidence in other cases. *And so there is given a science of things sensual*, although, as they are phenomena, there is not given a real intellection of them but only a logical intellection. Hence the sense is clear in which we are to suppose that science was denied in the case of phenomena by those who drew their inspiration from the Eleatic school.

SECTION III

On the principles of the form of the sensible world

§13

The principle of the form of the universe is that which contains the ground of the universal bond by which all substances and their states belong to the same whole which is called *a world*. The principle of the form of the *sensible world* is that which contains the ground of the *universal bond* of all things in as much as they are *phenomena*. The form of the *intelligible world* recognises an objective principle, that is some cause by which there is a binding together of things which exist in themselves. But the world in as much as it is regarded as a phenomenon, that is, in relation to the sensuality of the human mind, does not recognise any other principle of form than a subjective one, that is, a fixed law of the mind by which it is necessary that all the things which can be objects of the senses (through the quality of the senses) are seen *necessarily* to belong to the same whole. So whatever be the principle of the form of the sensible world, nevertheless its embrace is limited to *things actual* in so far as they are thought capable of *falling under the senses*. And so it embraces neither immaterial substances, which as such are already by definition altogether excluded from the external senses, nor the cause of the world. For since it is by it that mind itself exists and is active by means of any of its senses, this cause cannot be an object of the senses. These formal principles of the *phenomenal universe*, absolutely primary, catholic and moreover as it were schemata and conditions of anything sensitive in human cognition, I shall now show to be two, namely space and time.

§14

On time

1. *The idea of time does not arise from but is supposed by the senses.* For it is only through the idea of time that it is possible for the things which come before the senses to be repre- II 399 sented as being simultaneous or coming after one another. Nor does succession generate the concept of time, but it makes appeal to it. And so the notion of time regarded as though acquired through experience is very badly defined, when it is defined by means of the series of actual things which exist one *after* the other. For I do not understand the meaning of the little word *after*, except by means of the already previous concept of time. For those things come *after* one another which exist at *different times*, just as those things are *simultaneously* which exist *at the same time*.

2. *The idea of time is singular* and not general. For no time is thought of except as a part of the same one boundless time. If you think of two years you cannot represent them to yourself except in a determined position in relation to each other, and, if they should not follow one another immediately, except as joined to one another by some intermediate time. But among different times the time which is *earlier* and the time which is *later* cannot be defined in any way by some marks conceivable to the intellect, unless you were willing to enter upon a vicious circle, and the mind only discerns the distinction between them by a singular intuition. Moreover you conceive of all actual things as situated *in* time and not as contained *under* its general notion as under a common mark.

3. *The idea* therefore *of time is an intuition* and since it is conceived before every sensation, as the condition of relations met with in things sensible, it is not a sensual intuition but a *pure intuition.*

4. *Time is a continuous quantity* and is the principle of the laws of the continuous in the changes of the universe. For the continuous is a quantity which is not composed of things simple. But through time only relations are thought, without any entities being given in relation to one another, and so in time as a quantity there is composition and should this composition be conceived as wholly abolished it leaves nothing at all behind it. But if nothing at all is left of a composite when all composition has been abolished, then that composite is not composed of simple parts. Therefore, etc.[7] So any part at all of time is itself time, and the things which are in time, being simple things, I mean *moments*, are not parts of time, but *boundaries* with time between them. For when two moments are given, time is not given except in so far as in those moments actual things succeed one another. Therefore in addition to a given moment there must be given a time in whose later part there may be another moment.

Now the metaphysical law of *continuity* is as follows: *All changes are continuous* or flow, that is opposite states do not succeed one another except through an intermediate series of different states. For two opposite states are in different moments of time, but between the two moments there would always be some time intervening and in the infinite II 400 series of moments of that time the substance is not in one of the given states nor in the other and yet it is not in no state. And so the substance will be in different states and moreover it will be so to infinity.

The celebrated Kaestner, intending to subject this law of Leibniz to examination, challenges its defenders* to show that *the continuous movement of a point over all the sides of a triangle is impossible*, this being something which, if the law of continuity is granted, would unquestionably require proof. Here then is the demonstration asked for. Let the letters *abc* denote the three angular points of a rectilinear triangle. If something moveable passes in continuous motion over the lines *ab*, *bc*, *ca*, that is over the whole perimeter of the figure, it necessarily follows that it moves through point *b* in the direction *ab* and also through the same point *b* in the direction *bc*. But since these movements are diverse they cannot exist *simultaneously*. Therefore the moment of the presence of the moveable point at the vertex *b* in so far as it is moving in the direction *ab* is different from the moment of the presence of the moveable point at the same vertex *b* in so far as it is moving along direction *bc*. But between the two moments there is a time. Therefore the moveable point is present at the same point through some time, that is *it is at rest* and so does not proceed in continuous motion. And this is contrary to the hypothesis. The same demonstration is valid for motion along any straight lines enclosing an angle that can be given. Therefore, according to the doctrines of Leibniz, a body does not change its direction in a motion which is continuous, except along a line no part of which is straight, that is a curve.

5. *Time is not something objective and real*, nor is it a sub-

* *Höhere Mechanick*, p. 354.[8]

stance or an accident or a relation, but it is the subjective condition necessary by the nature of the human mind for co-ordinating with each other by a fixed law whatsoever things are sensible, and it is a *pure intuition*. For it is only through the concept of time that we co-ordinate alike substances and accidents whether according to their simultaneity or their succession. And so the notion of time, as being the principle of form, is older than the concepts of substance and accident. As for relations or respects of any kind, in so far as they confront the senses, I mean the question whether they are simultaneously or come after one another, these involve nothing else but positions to be determined in time either at the same point thereof or at different points.

Those who assert the objective reality of time either conceive of time as some continuous flux within existence, yet without anything existing (a most absurd fabrication!), as above all the philosophers of the English, or else they conceive of it as something real abstracted from the succession of internal states as is maintained by *Leibniz* and his followers. Now the falsity of the latter opinion clearly betrays itself by the vicious circle in the current definition of time. Moreover it completely neglects *simultaneity*,* the most important consequence of time. Consequently it thus throws into confusion all use of sound reason, because it does not

II 401

* *Simultaneous things* are not so because they do not succeed one another. For when succession is removed there is indeed abolished some conjunction which there was because of the series of time, but there does not immediately arise therefrom *another* true relationship such as is the conjunction of all of them at the same moment. For simultaneous things are joined together at the same moment of time just as successive things are joined together by different moments. So, though time be of one dimension only, yet the *ubiquity* of time (to speak with Newton), whereby *all* things sensitively thinkable are at *some time*, adds a further dimension to the quantity of actual things in as much as they hang as it were upon the same point of time. For if you were to describe time by a straight line produced to infinity and if you were to describe things simultaneous at any point of time by lines joining at right angles, the surface which is thus generated will represent the *phenomenal world* both as substance and as accidents.

postulate the determination of the laws of motion according to the measure of time, namely movement,[9] but postulates the determination of time itself, as regards its own nature, by means of things observed in motion or in any series of internal changes. And thereby all certitude of rules is utterly abolished. As for the fact that we could not estimate the *quantity* of time except in the concrete, namely either by *motion* or by *the succession of thoughts*, this fact arises because the concept of time rests only on an internal law of the mind and is not a certain intuition born with us. And so the action of the mind when it co-ordinates its own sensa would not be elicited without the help of the senses. Indeed so far is it from being the case that anyone has ever yet deduced from elsewhere and explained the concept of time with the help of the reason, that rather the principle of contradiction itself has the same concept as a premise and bases itself on the concept as its condition. For *A* and *not-A* are not *inconsistent* unless they are thought *simultaneously*, (that is at the same time) about the *same thing*. For *after one another* (that is at different times) they *can apply* to the same thing. Hence it is only in time that the possibility of changes is thinkable, and time is not thinkable because of changes but vice versa.

6. Now although *time* posited in itself and absolutely would be an imaginary entity, yet, in as much as it pertains to the immutable law of sensibles as such, it is a most veridical concept and a condition of intuitive representation extending to infinity over all possible objects of the senses. For since simultaneous things as such cannot come before the senses except with the help of time and changes are only thinkable through time, it is clear that this concept contains the universal form of phenomena. And so it is clear that all observable events in the world, all movements and all internal vicissitudes necessarily accord with the axioms to be known about time and which in part I have already II 402 expounded. For *it is only under these conditions that they can be objects of the senses and can be co-ordinated.* Accordingly it is contradictory to wish to arm reason against the first postu-

lates of pure time, for example continuity, etc. For they are the consequences of laws than which nothing prior and nothing older is found, and reason itself in using the principle of contradiction cannot dispense with the assistance of this concept, to such an extent is the concept primitive and original.

7. Time therefore is the *formal principle of the sensible world* which is absolutely first. For all things which are sensible, no matter how, cannot be thought unless either as simultaneous or as placed one after the other, and so as enfolded as it were by a period of unique time and related to one another by a determinate position. As a result there necessarily arises through this concept, which is primary to everything sensitive, a formal whole which is not a part of something else, that is the *phenomenal world*.

§15

On Space

A. *The concept of space is not abstracted from external sensations.* For I may not conceive of something as placed outside me unless by representing it as in a place which is different from the place in which I myself am, nor may I conceive of things outside one another unless by locating them in different places in space. Therefore the possibility of external perceptions as such *supposes* the concept of space and does not *create* it. In the same way also things which are in space affect the senses but space itself cannot be derived from the senses.

B. *The concept of space is a singular representation* comprehending all things *within itself*, not an abstract common notion containing them *under itself*. For what you speak of as *several places* are only parts of the same boundless space, related to one another by a fixed position, nor can you conceive to yourself a cubic foot unless it be bounded in all directions by the space that surrounds it.

C. *The concept of space is therefore a pure intuition.* For it is a singular concept, not conflated from sensations, but the fundamental form of all external sensation. Indeed it is easy to notice this pure intuition in the axioms of geometry and in any mental construction of postulates or even of problems. That there are not given in space more than three dimensions, that between two points there is only one straight line, that from a given point on a plane surface a circle can be described with a given straight line, etc.— these cannot be concluded from some universal notion of space, but can only be *seen* in space itself as in something concrete. Which things in a given space lie towards one quarter and which things incline towards the opposite quarter are things that cannot be described discursively or reduced to intellectual marks by any mental acuteness. Thus between solids which are perfectly similar and equal but not congruent, in which genus are the left hand and the right hand (in so far as they are conceived solely according to their extension), or spherical triangles from two opposite hemispheres, there is a diversity which makes it impossible for the boundaries of their extension to coincide although they could be substituted for one another as far as concerns all the things which may be expressed in marks intelligible to the mind in speech. And so it is clear that in these cases the diversity, I mean the discongruity, can only be noticed by a certain act of pure intuition. Hence geometry uses principles which are not only indubitable and discursive but come before the gaze of the mind, and the *evidence* in demonstrations (which is the clarity of certain cognition in so far as it is assimilated to sensual cognition) is not only greatest in geometry but is also the only evidence which is given in pure sciences and is the *exemplar* and means of all *evidence* in other sciences. For since geometry contemplates *relations of space* and the concept of space contains in itself the very form of all sensual intuition, nothing can be clear and perspicuous in things perceived by the external sense unless it be by the mediation of the same intuition the contem-

II 403

plation of which is the function of the science of geometry. But geometry does not demonstrate its own universal propositions by thinking an object by means of a universal concept as happens with things rational, but by subjecting it to the eyes by means of a singular intuition as happens with things sensitive.*

D. *Space is not something objective* and real, nor is it a substance or an accident, or a relation, but it is *subjective* and ideal and proceeds from the nature of the mind by an unchanging law, as a schema for co-ordinating with each other absolutely all things externally sensed. Those who defend the reality of space either conceive of it to themselves as an *absolute* and boundless *receptacle* of possible things, an opinion which finds favour with most geometers, following the English, or else they contend that it is the relation *itself* which obtains between existing things, which vanishes entirely when the things are taken away and can only be thought among things actual, as, following Leibniz, most of our own people maintain. As for that first empty fabrication of the reason, since it invents an infinite number of true relations without any entities related to one another, it pertains to the world of fable. But those who go off after the second opinion fall because of a far worse mistake. For the first group of people only set up a slight obstacle in the way of certain concepts which are rational or pertain to noumena and which are otherwise especially obscure to the intellect, for example questions about the spiritual world, about omnipresence, etc. But the second group are in

II 404

* It is easy to demonstrate that space must necessarily be conceived of as a continuous quantity and I here pass it over. But the result of this is that the simple in space is not a part but a boundary. Now a boundary is in general that in a continuous quantity which contains the ground of its limits. A space, which is not the boundary of another space, is *complete*[10] (*solid*). The boundary of a solid is *a surface*, of a surface a *line*, of a line *a point*. Therefore there are three sorts of boundaries in space, according as there are three dimensions. Of these boundaries two (surface and line) are themselves spaces. The concept of a *boundary* does not enter any other quantity but space or time.

headlong conflict with phenomena themselves and the most faithful interpreter of all phenomena, geometry. For without my bringing forward the obvious circle in the definition of space in which they are necessarily entangled, they throw down geometry from the summit of certitude and thrust it back into the rank of those sciences whose principles are empirical. For if all the affections of space are merely borrowed by experience from external relations, there is only a comparative universality present in the axioms of geometry, of the kind that is obtained by induction, that is, extending as far as it is observed. Nor is there present any necessity except in accordance with the established laws of nature nor any precision except what is arbitrarily constructed, and there is hope, as happens with things empirical, of uncovering sometime a space endowed with different primitive affections and perhaps even a rectilinear figure enclosed by two straight lines.

E. Although the *concept of space* as some objective and real entity or affection be imaginary, none the less *in relation to any things sensible whatsoever* it is not only *most veridical* but is also the foundation of all truth in external sensuality. For things cannot appear to the senses under any species at all except by the mediation of the power of the mind which co-ordinates all sensations according to a law which is stable and is planted in its own nature. Since, then, nothing at all can be given to the senses except in conformity with the primitive axioms of space and its consequences (so geometry teaches), whatever can be given to the senses will necessarily accord with these axioms even though their principle is only subjective. For it only accords with itself, and the laws of sensuality will only be laws of nature, *to the extent that it can come before the senses*. Accordingly nature is meticulously subjected to the precepts of geometry, as far as concerns all the affections of space there demonstrated, not upon an invented hypothesis but upon a hypothesis given intuitively, as the subjective condition of all the phenomena by which nature can ever be revealed to the senses.

Assuredly, had not the concept of space been given originally by the nature of the mind (in such a way that a person who strove to fashion with his mind any other relations than those dictated by this concept would be wasting his effort, because he would have been compelled to use this very con-

II 405 cept to support his own fiction), then the use of geometry in natural philosophy would be far from safe. For then it could be doubted whether this very notion of space derived from experience is sufficiently in accord with nature if perhaps the determinations from which it had been abstracted were denied. And indeed a suspicion of this has even entered the minds of some. *Space* therefore is the *formal principle of the sensible world*, absolutely first, not only because it is only[11] through its concept that the objects of the universe could be phenomena but above all for this reason, that by its essence space is nothing if not unique, embracing all things whatsoever which are externally sensible, and so it constitutes the principle of *entirety*, that is of a whole which cannot be a part of another whole.

Corollary

So here are the two principles of sensitive cognition, not general concepts as with things intellectual, but singular intuitions which are none the less pure. In these intuitions the parts and above all the simple parts do not, as the laws of reason teach, contain the ground of the possibility of a composite, but after the model of sensitive intuition *it is the infinite which contains the ground of each part* that can be thought and finally of the simple or rather of the *boundary*. For it is only when both infinite space and infinite time are given that any definite space and time are assignable by *limiting*. Moreover the point and likewise the moment cannot be thought in themselves, but are conceived of only in a space and time already given, as boundaries of that same space and time. Therefore all the primitive affections of these concepts are outside the barriers of reason and so cannot be explained intellectually in any way. None the less these concepts are *the substrates of the intellect*[12] when it draws consequences according to logical laws with the greatest possible certitude from primary things given intuitively. Indeed of these concepts *the one* properly concerns the intuition of an *object*, the other its *state*, especially its *representative* state. So space is also applied as a diagram to the concept of *time* itself, in representing time by a *line* and its boundaries (moments) by points. Time on the other hand more nearly *approaches* a *universal* and *rational concept*, by embracing with its own relations absolutely all things, namely space itself and in addition the accidents which are not included in spatial relations as being thoughts of the mind. Moreover time does not indeed dictate laws to the reason but all the same it does *constitute* the main *conditions thanks to which the mind may be able to compare its own notions according to the laws of reason*. So I can only be a judge of what is impossible when I predicate both *A* and *not-A* of the same subject *at the same time*. And particularly, if we apply the intellect to experience, the relation of cause and caused, at least in external objects, requires relations of space, but in all objects whether external or internal it is only with the assistance of the relation of time that the mind can be instructed as to what is earlier and what is later, that is what is cause and what is caused. And it is not open to us to make intelligible even the *quantity* of space itself unless we should express that space by a number after it has been related to a measure taken as a unity. This number itself only exists should there be a manifold[13] which is distinctly cognised by enumeration, that is by successively adding one to one in a given time.

Finally the question arises for everyone as though of its own accord whether each of the two *concepts* is *born with us* or *acquired*. The latter indeed already seems refuted by the things which have been demonstrated. The former however must not be so lightly admitted since it paves the road for a philosophy of the lazy, a philosophy which by citing the first cause declares any further research vain. But truly *each of the concepts* without any doubt *has been acquired*, not by abstraction from the sensing of objects indeed (for sensation gives the matter and not the form of human cognition), but from the very action of the mind, an action co-ordinating the mind's sensa according to perpetual laws, and each of the concepts is like an immutable diagram and so is to be cognised intuitively. For sensations excite this act of the mind but do not influence the intuition. Nor is there anything else here born with us except the law of the mind according to which it joins its own sensa together in a fixed manner as a result of the presence of an object.

SECTION IV

On the principle of the form of the intelligible world

§16

Those who take space and time for some real and absolutely necessary fastening as it were of all possible substances and states do not think that anything else is required in order to conceive how to a number of existing things there applies a certain original relation as the primitive condition of possible influxes and the principle of the essential form of the universe. For since whatever things exist are in their opinion necessarily somewhere, it appears superfluous to them to enquire why these same things are ready to hand for them in a fixed manner. For this, it seems to them, would be determined in itself by the entirety of a space which includes all things. But first of all this concept as has already been demonstrated would belong rather to the sensitive laws of a subject than to the conditions of objects themselves. And apart from that, even if you were to grant reality to the concept to the greatest possible extent, it still only denotes the intuitively given possibility of universal co-ordination. Accordingly the following question remains as intact as

II 407

before and only to be solved by the intellect, namely *what is the principle upon which this relation of all substances itself rests, a relation which when seen intuitively is called space*. This then is the point upon which hinges the question about the principle of the form of the intelligible world—to make clear how it is possible *that several substances should be in mutual interaction*[14] and upon this ground belong to the same whole which is called a world. We are not here contemplating the world as regards its matter, that is the natures of the substances of which it consists, as to whether they are material or immaterial, but the world as regards its form, that is how in general a bond obtains between several substances and a totality between all substances.

§17

Given several substances *the principle of the interaction* possible between them *does not consist in their existence alone*, but something else is required in addition whereby their mutual relations may be grasped by the intellect. For simply because of their subsistence they are not necessarily related to anything else unless perhaps the cause of themselves. But the relation of caused to cause is not interaction but dependence. Therefore if any interaction should intervene between them and other things there is needed a peculiar ground determining this interaction precisely.

And just in this consists the πρῶτον ψεῦδος (*primary error*)[15] of the theory of physical influx in the vulgar sense of that term, namely that it rashly assumes an interaction of substances and transeunt forces which are cognisable sufficiently by their existence alone and so it is not so much a system but rather the neglect of all philosophical system as superfluous in this argument. If we free this concept from that blemish we have a kind of interaction which is the only one which deserves to be called real and from which the whole constituted by the world deserves to be called real and not ideal or imaginary.

§18

A whole out of necessary substances is impossible. For the existence of each such substance is abundantly established apart
from any dependence upon anything else whatsoever, which
dependence does not enter into necessary things at all. And
II 408 so it is clear that not only does the interaction of substances
(that is, the reciprocal dependence of their states) not follow
from their own existence, but as being necessary substances
it is absolutely impossible for it to apply to them.

§19

So a whole of substances is a whole of contingents, and the
world, in its own essence, is composed of mere contingents. Moreover no necessary substance has a bond with the world
except as cause with caused, and accordingly not as a part
with its complements to the whole (since the bond of co-
parts is one of mutual dependence which dependence does
not enter into a necessary entity). Therefore the cause of the
world is an extramundane entity and so is not the soul of the
world nor is its presence in the world local but virtual.

§20

Mundane substances are entities from another entity, but not from a
diversity of entities—they are entities which are *all from one
entity.* For suppose they are the causal dependents of several
necessary entities: the effects whose causes are alien to any
mutual relation would not be in interaction. Therefore the
UNITY *in the conjunction of substances in the universe is a consequence of the dependence of all from one.* Hence the form of the
universe is witness to the cause of its matter, and only *the
unique cause of all things taken together is the cause of its entirety,*
nor is there any *architect* of the world who would not be at
the same time its *creator.*

§21

If there were several first and necessary causes with the things caused by them, their products would be *worlds*, not a *world*, since they would not be in any way connected to the same whole. And conversely if there were to be several actual worlds outside one another, then there are given several first and necessary causes, but in such a manner that neither is one world in interaction with the other nor is the cause of one world in any interaction with a world caused by the other cause.

Therefore several actual worlds outside one another *are not impossible simply because of the concept of such worlds* (as Wolff wrongly concluded from the notion of a complex or manifold which he thought was sufficient for a whole as such) but they are impossible only on this condition, namely *if there should exist only one necessary cause for all things*. If indeed several necessary causes were to be admitted, *there will be several worlds* which in the strictest metaphysical sense are *possible outside one another*.

§22

If, as the inference is valid from a given world to the ɪɪ 409 unique cause of all its parts, so also conversely the argument proceeded similarly from a given cause common to them all to the bond between them and so the form of the world (although I confess that this conclusion does not seem equally clear to me), then the primitive bond of substances would not be contingent but would be necessary because they are all *sustained by a common principle*, and so the harmony proceeding from their very subsistence, founded on their common cause, would proceed according to common rules. Now I call a *harmony* of this kind a harmony *established generally*. For a harmony which has no place except to the extent that any individual states of a substance whatsoever are adapted to the state of another would

be a *harmony established singularly*. And the interaction coming
from the first harmony would be real and *physical* while that
from the second would be ideal and *sympathetic*. So all the
interaction of the substances in the universe is *established
externally* (through the common cause of all of them) and is
either established generally by a physical influx (in its
more correct form) or negotiated for the states of the substances individually. But in this last case it is either founded
originally through the first constitution of any substance or
is impressed *on the occasion* of any change. Of these in turn
the first is called *pre-established harmony* and the second
occasionalism. And so if, as a result of all substances being
sustained by one being, the *conjunction* of all substances
whereby they form a unity were *necessary*, there will be a
universal interaction of substances through *physical influx* and
the world will be a real whole. But if not, the interaction
will be sympathetic (that is a harmony without true interaction) and the world will only be an ideal whole. For
myself, indeed, although it has not been demonstrated, none
the less the first of these alternatives has won approval
abundantly upon other grounds also.

Scholium

If it were permitted to take even a small step beyond the
boundaries of the apodeictic certitude which is appropriate
to metaphysics, it seems worth while to investigate certain
matters which pertain not only to the laws of sensitive
intuition but also to its causes which are to be known only
through the *intellect*. For indeed the human mind is not
affected by external things and the world is not open to
inspection by it to infinity, except *in as much as the mind
itself together with all other things is sustained by the same infinite
force of one being*. Hence the mind only senses external things
ii 410 through the presence of the same common sustaining cause.
And so space, which is the sensitively cognised universal
and necessary condition of the co-presence of all things, can

78

be called PHENOMENAL OMNIPRESENCE. (For the cause of the universe is not for that reason present to all and to individual things simply because it is in the places where they are. But there are places, that is, possible relations of substances, because it is present inwardly to all things.) Moreover the possibility of all changes and successions, of which possibility the principle, in so far as it is sensitively cognised, resides in the concept of time, supposes the per-durability of a subject whose opposed states follow in suc-cession, and that of which the states flow on does not endure unless it is sustained by another. And so it is the concept of time as a unique and unchangeable infinite* in which all things are and endure which is the *phenomenal eternity* of the general *cause*. But it seems more advisable to keep close to the shore of the cognitions granted to us by the medio-crity of our intellect rather than to put out into the deep sea of mystical investigations of that kind as Malebranche did. For his view is least distant from the one which is here being expounded, *namely that we intuit all things in God*.[16]

SECTION V

On method in metaphysics concerning things sensitive and things intellectual

§23

In all sciences whose principles are given intuitively, either by a sensual intuition (experience) or at least by an intuition which is sensitive but pure (concepts of space, time and number), that is, in natural science and in mathematics, *it is use which gives the method,* and it is by trying and finding out after the science has been brought to a certain ampli-tude and orderliness that it becomes clear what path and

---

* It is not moments of time that appear to succeed one another since then another time again would have to be premised for the succession of moments. But it is actual things which by sensitive intuition seem to descend as it were through the continuous series of moments.

79

what procedure one must pursue in order that it may be brought to fulfilment and shine the more purely when the blemishes both of mistakes and confused thoughts have been wiped away. Just in this way grammar after a more copious use of speech, and style after elegant examples of poems and orations, provided a handle for rules and discipline. But the II 411 *use* of the *intellect* in sciences of this kind, whose primitive concepts and axioms are given by sensitive intuition, is only the *logical* use, that is, the use by which we merely subordinate cognitions to one another according to their universality in conformity with the principle of contradiction, and we subordinate phenomena to more general phenomena, and subordinate the consequences of pure intuition to intuitive axioms. But in pure philosophy such as is metaphysics, in which the *use of the intellect* concerning principles is *real*, that is, the primitive concepts of things and of relations and the axioms themselves are given primitively by the pure intellect itself and not being intuitions are not immune from errors, *it is the method* which *comes before all science*, and everything which is attempted before the precepts of this method have been properly hammered out and firmly established is seen to have been rashly conceived and such that it must be rejected as being among the vain playthings of the mind. For since it is the right use of the reason which here sets up the very principles themselves and it is through its character alone that objects first become noticed and also the axioms which are to be thought about the objects, the exposition of the laws of pure reason is the very genesis of science and the distinction of these laws from supposititious laws is the criterion of truth. Hence as the method of this science may not be well known at the present time apart from the kind which logic teaches generally to all the sciences, and the method which is adapted to the singular character of metaphysics may be wholly unknown, it is no wonder that those who have devoted themselves to this research, appear, by rolling their own stone of Sisyphus unceasingly, to have made scarcely any progress at all up to the present time. Now although I have here neither the intention nor the opportunity of discoursing at greater length on such a distinguished and far-ranging theme, I shall all the same now briefly sketch out those things which constitute a part of this method which is not to be scorned, namely the *contagion of sensitive cognition with intellectual*, not only in as much as it creeps up upon the incautious in the application of principles but in as much as it also produces spurious principles in the guise of axioms.

§24

Every method of metaphysics concerning things sensitive and things intellectual comes back to this precept above all: great care must be taken *lest the domestic principles of sensitive cognition transgress their boundaries and affect things intellectual.* For the *predicate* in any judgement enunciated intellectually *is the condition* without which we assert that the subject is not thinkable and so the predicate would be a principle of cognising. Accordingly if the predicate is a sensitive concept it will only be the condition of a possible sensitive cognition and so it will square especially with the subject of a judgement whose concept is likewise sensitive. But if the predicate II 412 were to be applied to an intellectual concept, such a judgement will only be valid according to subjective laws. Hence the predicate is not to be predicated and stated objectively of an intellectual notion itself, but *only as the condition without which there is no place for the sensitive cognition of the given concept.** But since the illusions of the intellect, through the

* The use of this criterion is fertile and easy, in distinguishing principles which only enunciate laws of sensitive cognition from those which in addition teach something about the objects themselves. For should the predicate be an intellectual concept, its relation to the subject of the judgement, however much the subject be sensitively thought, always denotes a mark which applies to the object itself. But *should the predicate be a sensitive concept*, since the laws of sensitive cognition are not conditions of the possibility of things themselves, it will not be valid of the *intellectually thought subject* of a judgement, and so will be unable to be enunciated covert misuse of a sensitive concept as an intellectual mark, can be called (on the analogy of the accepted meaning of the term) *a fallacy of subreption*, the permutation of things intellectual and things sensitive will be the *metaphysical fallacy of subreption* (an *intellectuated phenomenon*, if a barbarous expression is pardoned). And so such a *hybrid* axiom which tries to sell things sensitive as being things that necessarily adhere to an intellectual concept is called by me a *subreptic axiom*. And from these spurious axioms indeed have proceeded principles for deceiving the intellect which have disastrously permeated the whole of metaphysics. But in order that we may have a criterion for these judgements which may be ready to hand and cognisable with clarity, and as it were a touchstone[17] by which we may distinguish them from genuine judgements and at the same time, should they perchance appear to be firmly attached to the intellect, a certain docimastic art with whose help a just appreciation could be made of how much pertains to things sensitive and how much to things intellectual, I am of the opinion that this is a question into which we must go more deeply.

§25

Here then is the PRINCIPLE OF REDUCTION for any subreptic axiom: *If of any intellectual concept whatsoever there is predicated generally anything which pertains to the relations of* SPACE AND TIME, *it must not be enunciated objectively and it only*
II 413 *denotes the condition without which a given concept is not cognisable sensitively.* That an axiom of this kind would be spurious and

---

objectively. So in the well-known popular axiom: *whatever exists is somewhere*, since the predicate contains the conditions of sensitive cognition, it will not be able to be enunciated generally of the subject of a judgement, namely of anything whatsoever which *exists*. And so this formula when it lays down precepts objectively is false. But should the proposition be converted so that the predicate became an intellectual concept, it will emerge as most true, namely: *whatever is somewhere exists.*

if not false at least rashly and precariously asserted is clear from the following: since[18] the subject of the judgement is conceived intellectually it pertains to the object, but the predicate since it contains determinations of space and time pertains only to the conditions of sensitive human cognition. And this cognition since it does not adhere necessarily to every cognition of the same object cannot be enunciated universally of a given intellectual concept. But that the intellect should be so easily subject to this fallacy of subreption results from the following: it is deluded by the authority of a certain other rule which is very true. For we rightly suppose that *whatever cannot be cognised by any intuition at all is thereby not thinkable* and so impossible. But since we cannot by any effort of the mind, not even by inventing it, obtain any other intuition than that which occurs in accordance with the form of space and time, it happens that we treat as impossible every intuition whatsoever which is not bound by these laws (leaving aside a pure intellectual intuition exempt from the laws of the senses, such as that which is divine, which Plato calls an idea). And so we subject all things which are possible to the sensitive axioms of space and time.

§26

But all the illusions of sensitive cognitions passing under the guise of cognitions that are intellectual, from which subreptic axioms arise, can be reduced to three species, for which take these as the general formulas:

1. The same sensitive condition under which alone the *intuition* of an object is possible is the condition of the *possibility* itself of the *object*.

2. The same sensitive condition under which alone *the things given can be collated with one another to form the intellectual concept of the object* is also the condition of the possibility itself of the object.

3. The same sensitive condition under which some *object*

met with can alone be *subsumed under a given intellectual concept* is also the condition of the possibility itself of the object.

§27

The subreptic axiom of the FIRST class is: *whatever is, is somewhere and at some time.* But by this spurious principle all II 414 entities, even if they were to be cognised intellectually, are bound in their existence by the conditions of space and time. Hence in the case of the places in the corporeal universe of immaterial substances (of which, however, for the same reason no sensitive intuition is given nor any representation under such a form), in the case of the seat of the soul and other cases of that kind empty questions are bandied about, and since things sensitive are improperly mixed with things intellectual like things square with things round, it usually happens that among the disputants one seems to be milking a he-goat and the other to be holding a sieve underneath.[19] But there is a presence of immaterial things in the corporeal world which is a virtual presence though not a local presence (although the latter is improperly but repeatedly asserted to be the case). Now space does not contain the conditions of possible mutual actions except for matter. And what constitutes the external relations of forces for immaterial substances, both relations among themselves and relations to bodies, completely escapes the human intellect, and this also the perspicacious Euler,

*Space and time are conceived as though they comprehend *in themselves* all the things which meet the senses in any way. So there is not given according to the laws of the human mind an intuition of any entity except as contained *in space and time*. With this prejudice one can compare another which properly is not a subreptic axiom but a sport of the phantasy which could be expressed in a general formula as follows: whatsoever exists, *in it is space and time*, that is, every substance is *extended* and continually *changed*. For although people whose concepts are somewhat crass are firmly bound by this law of the imagination, yet they themselves easily see that this only applies to the efforts of the phantasy to adumbrate for itself the species of things and does not apply to the conditions of existence.

in other matters a great investigator and judge of phenomena, acutely noted (in letters sent to a certain princess of
Germany[20]). Now when they come to the concept of a
surpeme being outside the world, it is impossible to express
the extent to which they are deluded by these shadows which
flit before the intellect. They fashion for themselves a *local
presence* of God and enfold God in the world as though he
were comprehended simultaneously in infinite space, intending to compensate for this limitation upon him, for-
sooth, by means of a locality conceived as it were *eminently*,
that is which is infinite. But it is absolutely impossible to be
in several places at the same time since different places are
outside one another and so what is in several places is outside itself and present to itself externally which is a contradiction. As for time, after they have not only exempted it
from the laws of sensitive cognition but have transferred it
beyond the boundaries of the world to the extramundane
being itself, as a condition of its existence, they involve
themselves in an inextricable labyrinth. Hence they torment
their spirits with absurd questions, for example why God
did not found the world many centuries back. They persuade themselves that it can indeed easily be conceived how
God sees things that are present, that is, actual *at the time at
which he is*. But how he sees in advance things which are to
be, that is, actual *at a time at which he not yet is*, this they II 415
think difficult to understand. (As if the existence of a necessary being were to descend successively through all moments
of imaginary time and when a part of his own duration had
already been exhausted he were to see in advance the eternity through which he was still to live, together with the
simultaneous events of the world.) All these problems vanish
like smoke when the notion of time has been rightly
discerned.

§28

Prejudices of the SECOND species conceal themselves to a
still greater extent. For they impose on the intellect through

sensitive conditions by which the mind is constrained if in certain cases it wishes to reach an intellectual concept. Of these prejudices one is that which affects the cognition of quantity, the other that which affects the cognition of qualities in general. The first is: *every actual manifold can be given numerically*, and so every quantity is finite. The second is: *whatever is impossible contradicts itself*. In each case the concept of time indeed does not enter into the notion itself of the predicate, and is not considered to be a mark of the subject, but all the same it serves as a means for giving form to the concept of the predicate and so as a condition it affects the intellectual concept of the subject in as much as it is only with its help that we reach the latter concept.

So, to take the case of the first prejudice, since every quantity and series whatsoever is only cognised distinctly through successive co-ordination, the intellectual concept of a quantity and a manifold arises only with the help of this concept of time, and it never reaches completion, unless the synthesis could be achieved in a finite time. Hence it is that an *infinite series* of co-ordinates could not be comprehended distinctly according to the limits of our intellect and so by the fallacy of subreption such a series would appear impossible. Certainly according to the laws of the pure intellect any series of things caused has its own *principle*, that is, there is not given in the series of things caused a regress which is without a boundary. But according to the sensitive laws any series of co-ordinates has its own assignable *beginning*. And these propositions, of which the second involves the *measurability* of the series and the first the *dependence* of the whole, are wrongly treated as identical. In like manner, to the *argument of the intellect* by which it is proved that given a substantial composite there would be given principles of composition, that is, things which are simple, there is added something *supposititious* covertly drawn from sensitive cognition, namely that in such a composite the regress in the composition of the parts would not be given to infinity, that is, that a definite number of parts would be given in any com-

86

posite whatsoever. And the sense of this second proposition is certainly not a twin to that of the first, and so it is rash to II 416 substitute it for the first. Therefore that the quantity of the world is limited (not the highest quantity), that it recognises a principle for itself, that bodies are composed of simple things, these can be known by a sign of the reason that is perfectly certain. But that the universe in its mass is mathematically finite, that its past duration can be given according to a measure, that there is a definite number of simple things constituting any body whatsoever, these are propositions which openly proclaim their source in the nature of sensitive cognition, and however much they can be treated as true in other respects, they suffer none the less from the undoubted blemish of their origin.

But as for what concerns the *second subreptic axiom*, that axiom arises by the rash conversion of the principle of contradiction. But the concept of time adheres to this primitive judgement to the extent that, when contradictory opposites are given *at the same time* about the same thing, there would clearly emerge an impossibility which is enunciated as follows: *whatever simultaneously is and is not is impossible.* Here since something is predicated by the intellect in a case which has been given according to sensitive laws, the judgement is especially true and most evident. But on the other hand if you were to convert the same axiom so that you were to say: *everything impossible simultaneously is and is not* or, involves a contradiction, you are predicating something generally, by virtue of sensitive cognition, about an object of the reason and so you are subjecting an intellectual concept about the possible or the impossible to the conditions of sensitive cognition, namely the relations of time. This indeed is most true for the laws by which the human intellect is constrained and limited but cannot in any way be conceded objectively and generally. For our intellect, at least, *does not notice an impossibility,* except when it can note a simultaneous enunciation of opposites about the same thing, that is only when a contradiction occurs. Therefore wherever such a condition

87

does not present itself, there no judgement about impossibility is open to the human intellect. But by treating the subjective conditions of judging as objective it is rashly concluded that for that reason it would not be permitted to any intellect at all and so, that *whatever does not involve a contradiction would be therefore possible.* Hence so many vain fabrications of *forces* I know not what invented at pleasure, which freed from the obstacle of inconsistency burst forth in a horde from any spirit which is architectonic or if you prefer it with a proclivity for chimaeras. For since a *force* is nothing else but the *relation* of a substance *A* to *something else B* (an accident) as of the ground to the grounded the possibility of each force *does not rest upon the identity* of cause and caused or of substance and accident. And so also the impossibility of falsely fabricated forces *does not depend upon contradiction alone.* So it is not permitted to take any *original force* as possible unless *it has been given by experience,* nor can its possibility be conceived a priori by any perspicacity of the intellect.

II 417

§29

Subreptic axioms of the THIRD species issuing from conditions proper to a *subject,* from which conditions they are rashly transferred to *objects,* do not proliferate in such a way that (as happens with those which are of the second class) it is through *things given sensitively* that the sole way lies open to the intellectual concept, but they proliferate because it is only with their help that an intellectual concept can *be applied to a case given* by experience, that is, it can be cognised whether something is contained under a fixed intellectual concept or not. Of this kind is the trite saying in certain schools: *whatever exists contingently, at some time did not exist.* This supposititious principle arises from the poverty of the intellect which usually sees clearly the *nominal* marks of contingency or necessity, but rarely the *real* marks. Hence whether the opposite of some substance is possible, since it can hardly be seen clearly by marks secured a priori, will not be known from any other source except *it be established that at some time the substance was not in existence*. And changes are truer witnesses of contingency than contingency is of changeability so that if we met with nothing in the world which was fluid and transitory it would be with difficulty that any notion of contingency would arise for us. And so although the direct proposition is most true, that *whatever at some time was not is contingent*, its inverse only indicates the conditions under which alone it is permitted to discern whether something exists necessarily or contingently. And so should it be enunciated as a subjective law (which it really is), it ought to be expressed as follows: *when it is not established that something has at some time not been in existence sufficient marks of its contingency are not given by common intelligence*. This in the end tacitly passes into an objective condition as though without this being added there would be no place for contingency at all. This done, there arises an axiom which is counterfeit and erroneous. For this world, although existing contingently, *is sempiternal*, that is, simultaneous with every time, so that it is therefore wrong to assert that there has been some time at which it did not exist.

§30

There are also certain other principles in addition to the subreptic principles, and with a great affinity to them. These indeed do not rub off any taint of sensitive cognition onto a given intellectual concept but all the same the intellect is so deluded by them that it takes them for arguments II 418 drawn from an object, although they are only commended to us by their *convenience* with[21] the free and ample use of the intellect according to its singular nature. And so, just as the principles which have been enumerated by us above, they rest upon *subjective* grounds, not in truth on the laws of sensitive cognition, but on the laws of intellectual cognition itself, namely the conditions under which it seems to the intellect easy and practicable to use its own perspicacity. Let me insert some mention of these principles here in place of a conclusion, principles which, so far as I know, have not yet been distinctly expounded elsewhere. Now I call *principles of convenience*[21] those rules of judging to which we gladly submit ourselves and to which we cling as axioms, for the sole reason that *if we depart from them scarcely any judgement about a given object would be permitted to our intellect.* In this group come the following. The FIRST is that by which we suppose that *all things in the universe take place in accordance with the order of nature.* This principle indeed Epicurus professes without any restriction, but all philosophers profess it with one voice, subject only to the rarest exceptions and ones only to be admitted under extreme necessity. But we so decide not because we possess such ample cognition of the events in the world according to the common laws of nature nor because either the impossibility or the very slight hypothetical possibility of things supernatural was apparent to us, but because, if you depart from the order of nature, the intellect would have no use at all, and the ill-considered citation of things supernatural is the couch upon which reclines a lazy intellect. For the same reason, *comparative miracles*, namely influxes of spirits, we carefully keep out of the exposition of phenomena. For since their nature is to us unknown the intellect would be turned aside to its own great detriment, away from the light of experience by which alone it has the opportunity of procuring for itself the laws of judging, towards shadows of species and causes to us unknown. The SECOND principle *is* that *leaning towards unity* which is proper for the philosophical spirit and from which has flowed that very well-known canon: *principles are not to be multiplied beyond what is absolutely necessary.* To this we give our vote not because either by reason or experience we clearly see a causal unity in the world, but we pursue that very unity driven on by our intellect which seems to itself to have been successful in the explanation of phenomena only to the degree that it has received permission to descend from the same principle to the very large number of things grounded. The THIRD of the principles of this kind is: *No matter at all comes into being or passes away* and all the vicissitudes of the world concern its form alone. This postulate, at the instigation of the common intellect, is spread abroad through all the schools of philosophers, not because it has been taken as discovered or demonstrated by arguments a priori, but because, if you admit matter itself II 419 as in flux and transitory, nothing at all would be left which was stable and durable which might more fully promote the explanation of phenomena according to universal and perpetual laws and in this way promote the use of the intellect.

So much on method, especially concerning the distinction between sensitive and intellectual cognition. If some day this method is given an exact expression by a more careful investigation, it will serve as a propaedeutic science which will be of immense service to all who intend to penetrate the very recesses of metaphysics.

NOTE. Since in this last section it is the search for a method which occupies every page and since the rules which teach us the true form of arguing about things sensitive shine with their own light and do not borrow it from examples brought forward for the sake of illustration, I have inserted a mention of these examples only as it were in passing. Accordingly it is not strange that to the majority of people some things there will seem to have been asserted with more audacity than truth, and when on some occasion it is permissible to be more prolix they will certainly demand for themselves a greater weight of arguments. Thus what I have adduced in §27 on the locality of immaterial things needs explanation, which please seek in Euler, l.c., vol. II, pp. 49–52.[22] For the soul is not in interaction with the body because it is detained in a certain place in the body, but there is attributed to it a determined place in the universe because it is in mutual interaction with a certain body, and when this interaction is broken off all its position in space is destroyed. And so its *locality* is *derivative* and is bestowed upon it contingently and is *not a primitive* and necessary condition adhering to its existence. For all things which in themselves cannot be objects of the external senses (such senses as man possesses), that is, *immaterial things,* are absolutely exempted from the universal condition of *things sensible externally,* namely space. Hence the absolute and immediate locality of the soul can be denied and yet a hypothetical and mediate locality assigned to it.

IV

*Selections from Kant's correspondence with Lambert,
Sulzer, Mendelssohn, and Herz (1770–79)*

Letter 1 (LVII)   *13 October 1770*

From JOHANN HEINRICH LAMBERT[1]

Noble Sir,   x 98
Your noble letter, along with your treatise on the sensible
and intelligible world, was a source of no small pleasure to
me, particularly since I am obliged to regard the latter as a
proof of how metaphysics, and thus ethics as well, can be x 99
improved. I very much hope that the position offered to
you, Noble Sir, may give occasion to further such essays,
unless you resolved to publish them separately.

You remind me, Noble Sir, of the remark, made five
years ago now, *about perhaps undertaking future researches
jointly.* At the time, I wrote making this suggestion to Herr
Holland, and would have written eventually to some other
scholars had it not been for the fact that the Leipzig Book
Fair Catalogue showed that belles-lettres were crowding out
everything else. I think, however, that it is a passing phase
and that a return will again be made to more solid learning.
Some at the universities who have only read poetry, novels
and literary writings have already confessed to me here
that, when they came to take over business, they found
themselves in an entirely strange land and had to start
studying, as it were, from the beginning again. Such as they
can give very good advice about what ought to be done at
the universities.

In the mean time, my plan was partly to write a supply of

short papers myself, and partly to invite some scholars of a similar turn of mind to do the same. In this way, I hoped to set up, as it were, a private society, where everything which all too easily corrupts public learned societies *would be avoided*. The proper members would have been a small number of select philosophers, conversant however at the same time with physics, and mathematics.

For in my opinion a metaphysician pure and simple is constituted as if he lacked a sense, in the way that a blind man lacks the sense of sight. Members of this society would have communicated to each other their writings, or at least an adequate idea of them, in order to help each other, if need be, in cases where two heads are better than one. Had each, however, remained true to his own opinion, each would have been able, with suitable modesty and conscious of his own fallibility, to get his own opinion published. Philosophical papers, as well as papers on linguistics and belles-lettres, would have been the most frequent. Papers on physics and mathematics would possibly have been accepted as well, especially where they bordered on the philosophical.

x 100   The first volume would have had to have been excellent, and because of the contributions that were to be expected, the right would always have been reserved of returning, if necessary, such papers as the majority opposed. In difficult matters the members would have been able to communicate their opinions to each other tentatively, or in such a fashion as to leave room for objections and rejoinders.

You could still indicate to me now, Noble Sir, to what extent you regard such a society as a real possibility, that could, if need be, be lasting. In this connection, I take the *Acta Eruditorum*[2] as an example—the *Acta Eruditorum* as the exchange of letters that it originally was between some of the greatest scholars; the *Bremische Beiträge*[3]—where the original poets *Gellert*,[4] *Rabener*,[5] *Klopstock*,[6] etc., made their efforts known in those days, and at the same time improved themselves—could serve as a second example. The purely philosophical seems to involve several difficulties. But it would of course depend on a good choice of members. The writings would have to be free from everything heretical or too capricious and trifling.

Meanwhile, I have a number of papers that could have been contributed to such a collection. Some of them have been given to the *Acta Eruditorum*; some I have read to the Academy here. On other occasions I have also communicated ideas suitable for treatment in such papers. Now, however, I turn to your excellent treatise, since you particularly want to know my opinion on it. If I have rightly understood the matter, it contains a number of basic propositions, which I shall here give as briefly as possible.

The first main proposition is this: insofar as *human* knowledge is, in part, *knowledge* and, in part, has a form peculiar to itself, it divides into the traditional phenomenon and noumenon. According to this division, human knowledge takes its origin from two quite different, and so to say, heterogeneous sources. What originates from the one source can never be derived from the other. Knowledge proceeding from the senses is and remains, therefore, sensible, just as knowledge that proceeds from the understanding remains in character peculiar to its origin.

In my opinion, the problem raised in this proposition is chiefly one of *generality*. To what extent, namely, are these two kinds of knowledge so completely separate, that they *nowhere* meet. Should this be proved *a priori*, then it must x 101 be done by appealing to the nature of sense and the nature of understanding. But since we must first become acquainted with them *a posteriori*, the problem becomes one of classifying and enumerating objects.

This seems also to be the method you have adopted, Noble Sir, in the 3rd section. In this respect, it seems quite correct to me that what is *temporally* and *spatially* bound offer truths of quite a different kind from those which must be regarded as eternal and unchanging. I have merely noted this in Alethiol. §§81, 87. Important as it may be in itself, it is not so easy to understand the reason why truths are temporally and spatially bound in the way they are and not differently.

Besides, there the discussion was only about existing things. Geometrical and chronometrical truths, however, are temporally and spatially bound, not by accident, but quite essentially. And insofar as the *concepts* of time and space are eternal, geometrical and chronological truths belong among those that are eternal and unchanging.

Now, you ask, Noble Sir, whether these truths are sensible. I can well concede this. It seems that the difficulty contained in the concepts of time and place can be discussed without considering this other question. The first four sentences of §14 seem to me to be quite correct. It is particularly good that in the fourth sentence you penetrate, Noble Sir, to the true concept of *continuity*, a concept that in metaphysics seems to be as good as completely lost, because of the wish to apply it absolutely, in connection with a complex of simple entities, and it had thus to be modified. Now, the difficulty really lies in the 5th sentence. It is certainly true, Noble Sir, that you do not offer the sentence *Time is a subjective condition etc.*[7] as a definition. But nevertheless it is intended to indicate something that is peculiar and essential to time. Time is indisputably a necessary condition and thus belongs to the representation of sensible things and of all things temporally and spatially bound. It is necessary, in particular, to man in this representation. It is also a pure intuition; it is not a substance; it is not a mere relation. It differs from *duration*, as *place* differs from *space*. It is a special determination of duration. It is also not an accident, that disappears with substance etc. These propositions may all be correct. They do not lead to a definition, and perhaps the best definition will be, after all, in the end, that time is time. In this way it is not defined—and that in a most doubtful fashion—in terms of its relations to things that exist in time, thus committing at the same time the vicious circle fallacy. Time is a more determinate concept than *duration*, thus implying more negative propositions, e.g., what exists

x 102

96

in time has duration, but not the other way round, when one demands for *temporal* existence a beginning and an end. Eternity is not in time, for its duration is absolute. In the same way, a substance which has an absolute duration does not exist in time. Everything that exists has duration, but not everything exists in time, etc. With such a clear concept as that of *time*, there is no lack of propositions. The point seems chiefly to be that one must not define, but merely think, time and duration. All changes are temporally bound and cannot be thought without time. *If changes are real, so is time.* And this may after all be the case. *Should time not be real then no change is real.* However it seems to me that even an idealist must admit that changes really do take place and exist, at least, in his own representations, such as their beginning and ceasing. But having admitted this, time cannot be regarded as *other* than real. Time is not a substance etc., but a finite determination of duration. Time, with duration, has something real, whatever this may after all consist in. If it cannot be designated with any name derived from other things without danger of misunderstanding, it must either receive a newly constituted primitive term for its name; or it must remain nameless. What is real in time and space seems to have about it something simple and, with regard to everything else, heterogeneous, so that it can only be thought, not defined. Duration seems to be inseparable from existence. Whatever exists has duration either absolutely or for a time; and again, what has duration must really exist as long as it has duration. Existing things whose duration is not absolute are temporally ordered, insofar as they begin, continue, change and cease, etc. *Since I cannot deny reality to change,* until I am convinced to the contrary, I am still unable to say that time and thus space as well are both merely expedients for the benefit of human representations. Furthermore with respect to the x 103 ordinary way of talking about time in common parlance, it is always good to note the ambiguities that the word '*time*' has. For example:

97

'*A long time*' is an interval of time or of two moments and signifies a determinate duration.

'*About this time*', '*at this time*' etc. is either a definite instant, like the time of immersion and emersion in astronomy etc., or an indeterminate duration, of greater or shorter length, either preceding or succeeding a given instant, or a moment of time, etc.

You will now easily guess, Noble Sir, how I think with respect to place and space. Setting aside the ambiguities of the words, I lay down the following analogy with the greatest rigour:

$$\text{Time : duration} = \text{Place : space.}$$

The only differentiation that I make between them is that space has three dimensions, while duration has only one. In addition to this, each of these concepts has something peculiar to itself. Space, like duration, has something absolute and finite determinations as well. Space, like duration, has a reality peculiar to itself, which cannot be stated nor defined in terms of words derived from other things, without danger of misunderstanding. It is something simple and must be thought. The whole intelligible world is non-spatial, but it has a similitude of space easily distinguished from physical space. It is perhaps closer than a merely metaphorical similarity to physical space.

Theological difficulties which have rendered the doctrine of space a prickly one, especially since the time of *Leibniz* and *Clarke*,[8] have not yet led me astray with regard to this matter. In my opinion, complete success lies rather in leaving indefinite things which cannot be made clear. Moreover, I did not wish, while I was engaged on ontology, to keep glancing furtively at the succeeding parts of metaphysics. I have no objections at all to time and space being regarded merely as pictures and appearances. For leaving aside the fact that constant appearance is truth for us, whereby what is fundamental is either never discovered at all or only in the future, it is useful in ontology to discuss the concepts, as well, that are borrowed from appearance, *since ontological theory must, in the last analysis, be applied again to the phenomena.* For the astronomer, as well, begins with phenomena, derives his theory of the structure of the universe from them, and applies it, in his astronomical almanac, to the appearances and their prediction. In metaphysics, where the problem of appearance is so important, the astronomer's method will probably be the safest. The metaphysician can accept everything as appearance, can separate the empty from the real, and from the real he can infer the true. Should he proceed well in this way few will contradict him on account of his principles, and, in general, he will be applauded. Only it seems that time and patience are required to do this.   x 104

With regard to the fifth section I will now be brief. I should regard it as something very important if you could find, Noble Sir, a means of penetrating more deeply to the foundation and origin of those truths that are spatially and temporally bound. Insofar as this section is concerned with method, however, I need here only repeat what I have already said about time. For if change and with it time and duration as well are something real, it seems to follow that *the division suggested in the 5th section would have to have different and, in part, more nearly determinate, purposes.* The classification may then have to be differently drawn up as well, so as to accord with these changes. I thought this at §§25, 26. With respect to §27, the statement *Whatever is, is somewhere and somewhen* is partly mistaken and partly ambiguous, if it means *in space and time.* What has duration absolutely, is not in time, and the intelligible world is only in space, in the earlier mentioned sense of a similitude of space, or in the sense of intelligible space.

What you say, Noble Sir, in §28, as also in the note on pages 2 and 3, about mathematical infinity, that it has been corrupted in metaphysics by definitions and that a different notion has been substituted for it, has my complete approval. With respect to *the simultaneous being and not being* mentioned in §28, I think that a similitude of time occurs also in the intelligible world and the *simultaneous* is thus derivative, when it occurs in connection with proofs of absolute truths not spatially nor temporally bound. I should have thought that the *similitude of space and time* in the intelligible world could quite well be taken into consideration in your intended theory. It is a facsimile of real space and time, and can be quite easily differentiated from them. In symbolic knowledge we have, in addition, something intermediate between perception and truly pure thought. If we proceed correctly in designating what is simple and what the manner of composition is, we get reliable rules for discovering signs of compounds so complex that, although they can no longer be thought, nevertheless we are assured that the designation represents the truth. No one has yet succeeded in clearly imagining all the members of an infinite series simultaneously; and no one will ever do so in the future. That we calculate with such series, however, that we can give the sum of such a series, etc. is possible by virtue of the laws of symbolical knowledge. By this means we reach far beyond the limits of our actual thoughts. The symbol $\sqrt{-1}$ represents an inconceivable absurdity, and yet it can well be used for discovering theorems. What are generally regarded as proofs of pure understanding should in most cases be regarded as proofs of symbolical knowledge. I said this in §122 of my *Phenomenology*,[9] on the occasion of the question in §119. I have nothing, Noble Sir, against your making the note in §10 completely general.

x 105

I will now end my letter and leave you to do as you please with what I have written, Noble Sir. I have, however, one request: that you examine exactly the sentences that have been underlined in this letter.* And if you should wish to devote time to this purpose, let me know your opinion, without regard to the cost of postage. So far, I have been unable to deny all reality to time and space, nor have I been able to make them into mere pictures and appear-

* The underlined sentences have been italicised.—Transl.

ances. All change, I think, would have to be mere appearance. This would be contrary to one of my chief principles (§54 *Phenomenology*). If change is therefore real, then I attribute to time a reality as well. Changes succeed each other, begin, continue, cease etc.—all expressions derived from time. If you can teach me differently in this matter, Noble Sir, I do not think I would be much the loser. Time and space would be real appearance, whereby something would underlie this appearance, this something conforming exactly and constantly to the appearance,—as exact and constant as geometrical truths can ever be. The language of appearance will thus serve as exactly as the unknown true language. But I must say, that an appearance that simply never leads astray in this manner, may well be something more than mere appearance.

I presume that the *Haude-und Spenersche Zeitung*[10] will x 106 probably reach Königsberg from here. I shall, therefore, only briefly touch on the fact that I have been occasioned to inform the public, in Nr. 116 of 27 September of the current year, that someone has already been found to extend the table of divisors of numbers up to 204,000, and, if necessary, further still,—the table is in *the appendices to my logarithmic and trigonometric tables*,—and that someone else has undertaken to calculate the hyperbolic logarithms to many decimal places. I have given notice of this fact so as to obviate the duplication of this work at any time, so that the calculation of those still entirely incompleted tables should be undertaken. Now and again one comes across lovers of mathematics who enjoy calculating. I have reason to hope that the invitation,—which will also appear in the *Allgemeine Deutsche Bibliothek*,[11] in the *Göttingsche Anzeige*[12] and in the *Leipziger gelehrte Zeitung*[13] will not be fruitless. Should you, Noble Sir, find someone in your locality inclined to such calculations, I should be very pleased. A publisher does not pay for the time and trouble, according to merit, indeed, and I shall have difficulty getting more than a ducat a sheet. However, whatever the success may be, I request nothing for myself, and each will be able to draw his share, if necessary, from the publisher personally. Incidentally, the person who first presents himself for the calculation of the still incompleted tables, will, as is normal, once he has produced a proof of his ability, have the choice. Thus I have already given the choice to someone who offered himself privately and who will either do the calculations himself, or get someone to do them. Perhaps the table of numerical divisors will rise to 1,000,000 and by itself may constitute two octavo volumes.

> With true respect,
> I have the honour of being,
> Noble Sir,
> Your most devoted servant,
> J. H. Lambert.

Berlin 13 October 1770.

Letter 2 (LVIII)   *8 December 1770*

From JOHANN GEORG SULZER[14]

x 106 Noble, honoured Sir,

You have greatly obliged me by sending me your Inaugural Disputation, and with it you bestow on the public an im-
x 107 portant gift. I think I have already appreciated that much with certainty, although the conjunction of many affairs with my daily work on my book on the fine arts, now being printed, has not permitted me to grasp completely all the important concepts, that are to be found in considerable numbers, in your work. If you are willing to take the trouble to completely develop each of these concepts separately and to show the application of each in some detail, you will, I think, give a new impetus to philosophy.

These concepts seem to me not only fundamental but also very important. In only one small detail have I been unable to conform to your way of representing these matters. Until now, I have held *Leibniz's* concepts of time and space for correct; for I hold time to be different from duration, and space to be different from extension. Duration and extension are absolutely simple concepts not permitting of clarification, yet having, in my opinion, true reality. Time and space, however, are compound concepts that cannot be thought unless one has at the same time the concept of order. I have long imagined the natural influence of the substances and felt its necessity in roughly the same way as you; and I have notions on the distinction between sensible and intelligible, the clearness of which can be developed fairly extensively, as I have planned to show in detail, once I have the time to do so. But you will certainly anticipate me in these matters, Noble Sir, and this will please me very much. For at the moment, I really have little time, and indeed little disposition to work at such abstract matters, occupied as I am with work of an entirely different nature.

I had really hoped to learn from you whether we can hope soon to see your work on the metaphysic of morals. This work is of the highest importance for the theory of morals, which is still so unstable. I also have attempted something of this kind, in that I have undertaken to answer the question, in what consists the physical and psychological difference between what we call a virtuous soul and one that is vicious. I have sought to discover the real dispositions to virtue and vice in the first expressions of the imagination and feelings. I think this enquiry has been undertaken the x 108 less in vain in that it has led me to fairly simple and easily grasped concepts, which can be applied with ease and directness to the fields of education and upbringing. But at the moment I cannot execute this work either.[15]

I wish you sincerely, Noble Sir, good fortune in the glorious career which you have already started for yourself, and thereby health and leisure to complete it with honour.

F. G. Sulzer.

Berlin 8 December 1770

Letter 3 (LIX)   *25 December 1770*

From MOSES MENDELSSOHN[16]

x 108 Noble Sir,

Especially honoured Professor,

Herr *Marcus Herz*[17] who, through your teaching and still more, as he himself assures me, through your wise society, made himself a philosopher, proceeds laudably in that career which he first began to pursue under your eyes. Whatever my friendship can contribute to his progress will not be lacking to him. I love him sincerely and have the pleasure of enjoying his entertaining society almost every day. Nature, it is true, has done much for him. He possesses a clear understanding, a gentle heart, a moderated imagination and a certain subtlety of spirit which seems natural to his nation. But what good fortune it was for him that these very gifts of nature were so early led to the path of truth and goodness. How many have there been who have not had this good fortune, but have been left to themselves in the immeasurable space of truth and error; how many have thus had to consume the prime of their lives and their best energies in a hundred futile efforts, so that in the end both time and energy have been lacking to proceed on the way which they had at last, after long groping around, discovered. Would that I had had before my twentieth year a *Kant* for friend!

I took up your dissertation with the greatest eagerness and read it through with much pleasure, in spite of the fact that for many a long day, because of my weakened nervous system, I have scarcely been in the position to read through reflectively anything speculative of this value with the appropriate effort. Clearly, this little paper is the fruit of very long meditations and must be regarded as a constituent part of a complete system, which is peculiar to the author and of which the author is willing to show only a few examples, for the time being. The apparent obscurity itself which remains at certain points betrays to the experienced reader the relation to a whole, which has not yet been laid before him. Meanwhile, it is to be wished in the best interests of metaphysics, which regrettably has now fallen on bad times, that you should not long withhold from us the store of your meditations. Human life is short, and while we continually have the intention of making it still better, how easily the end surprises us. And again, why are you so afraid of repeating what you have already said. In connection with your own original thoughts, even the familiar appears from a new angle, offering prospects of which one had, until that moment, not thought. Furthermore, since you possess in an exceptional degree the gift of writing for many readers, it is hoped that you will not always limit yourself to the few adepts, who have eyes only for what is new and the skill to infer from the half-said what has not been said.

Since I do not quite count myself among these adepts I do not dare to communicate to you all the thoughts that your dissertation has occasioned in me. Permit me to set down here those thoughts alone which rather concern the incidental comments than the chief ideas.

Page 2, 3.—In the second edition of my *Philosophical Writings*[18] which is now printing and of which I shall have the honour to send you a copy, are to be found thoughts similar to yours on the infinite in extended magnitude, although my ideas are not so penetratingly argued as yours. Herr *Herz* can attest that everything was already prepared for the press when I first saw your paper. I also immediately expressed my pleasure to him, that a man of your importance should be in agreement with me on this point.

Page 11. You number Lord *Shaftesbury*[19] among those who follow *Epicurus*, at least at a distance.[20] Until now I have always believed that the moral instinct of the Earl was to be carefully distinguished from *Epicurus*' sensual pleasure. For the English philosopher, the former is an inborn x 110 faculty of distinguishing good and bad by mere feeling, whereas for *Epicurus* sensual pleasure is supposed to be, not merely a criterion of goodness, but itself the supreme good.

Page 15. 'What does the little word after mean' etc.[21] The difficulty seems to prove more the poverty of language than the incorrectness of the concept. The little word 'after' signifies indeed originally a temporal succession. But one can also give a general indication of the order by means of it, where two real things A and B are present, and where A can only exist when or while B does not exist. In a word, the order in which two things, either absolutely or hypothetically contradictory can yet be present. You will say that the words *when* and *while*, which I cannot help using, presuppose once more the idea of time. Very well! We want to avoid this little word as well then, since you think so I begin with the following definition:

A and B are both real and are the immediate (or, alternatively, equidistant) consequences (*rationata*) of a single ground C. I call them hypothetically compatible things (*compossibilia secundum quid*); should they, however, not be equidistant consequences or *rationata*, I call them hypothetically incompatible.

Now I continue:

The hypothetically compatible things (things which also in this world are compossibilities) are simultaneous, *simultanea*; the hypothetically incompatible actual things, however, succeed each other, and it is the nearer consequence (*rationatum*) which precedes, and the distant one which follows.

Here, I hope, no word occurs which presupposes the idea of time. In any case, it will be more in the language than in the thoughts.

There are several reasons why I cannot persuade myself that time should be something merely subjective. Succession is, after all, at least a necessary condition of the representations of finite minds. Now, finite minds are not merely subjects but also objects of representations, both of God and of their fellow-minds. Consequently succession is also to be regarded as something objective.

Furthermore, since we have to attribute a succession to

beings that have representations, and to the changes that they undergo, why not attribute succession to the sensible objects in the world as well, the pattern and prototype of representations.

Page 17. I do not understand how you find a vicious circle in this manner of conceiving time.[22] Time, is, according to Leibniz, a phenomenon, and, like all appearances, has something objective and something subjective. The subjective element is the *continuity*, thereby represented; the objective element, on the other hand, is the succession of changes, that are consequences equidistant from a ground.

Page 23.[23] I do not think that the condition 'at the same time' is as necessary as all that in the statement of the Law of Contradiction. Insofar as the subject is the same, A and not-A cannot be asserted of it, even at different times. The concept of the impossible requires no more than that *the selfsame subject should have two predicates*. A and not-A. One can also say: it is impossible that not-A be the predicate of the subject A.

I would not have presumed to be so bold, Noble Sir, as to judge your paper with such frankness as this, had not Herr *Herz* brought me to recognise your truly philosophical temper, and given me the assurance that you are very far from resenting such candour. This character is so rarely found among unoriginal imitators that it is, indeed, commonly a distinguishing sign of an independent mind. He who has personally experienced how difficult it is to find the truth and to convince oneself that one has found it, is at all times more inclined to tolerate those who think differently from himself.

> I have the honour to be,
> with the most complete respect,
> Noble Sir,
> the most obliging and devoted servant
> of my honoured professor.
> Moses Mendelssohn.

Berlin 25 December 1770.

Letter 4 (LXII)   *7 June 1771*

To MARCUS HERZ[17]

x 116 Most worthy friend,

What do you think of my negligence in corresponding? And what does your mentor Herr *Mendelssohn* and Prof. *Lambert* think of it? These honest people must certainly think that I must be a very rude person to repay so badly the trouble they have taken in their letters. And if they were to resolve for the future never again to allow themselves to be coaxed into this trouble, I could, of course, not blame them. But, if the inner difficulty one personally feels could become as obvious to other eyes, I hope you would suppose anything in the world as the cause of my silence, rather than indifference or a lack of respect. Please, then, relieve these worthy men of such a suspicion or prevent their entertaining it. For the same hindrance that has caused my delay is even now still preventing my reply. Without counting the bad habit of regarding tomorrow's post as more convenient than today's, there are really two causes for my silence. Letters, such as those with which these two scholars have honoured me, lead me into a long series of researches. You know that I do not merely regard rational objections from the standpoint of their refutability, but that I weave them,

x 117 in reflection, into the web of my own judgements and give them the right of upsetting all the opinions I had previously formed and formerly cherished. I hope, by always regarding my judgements impartially from the viewpoint of others, to derive some third position superior to the previous ones. Moreover, even the mere lack of conviction in men of such insight is always for me a proof that my theories are deficient in clearness at least, or even in some more essential respect. Now, long experience has taught me that force cannot obtain, nor effort hasten, an understanding of the matters we propose to study. On the contrary, a fairly lengthy period of time is necessary for a single concept to be examined intermittently, in all kinds of relationship and in contexts as extensive as possible; and above all, in addition, to test whether one's conclusions hold good against the sharpest doubt so that, in the course of these reflections, the sceptical spirit may awaken within one. In this intention, I have, I think, put to good use the time which I have allowed myself, thus running the danger of earning the reproach of impoliteness, although I have in fact remained silent out of respect for the judgement of these two scholars. You know what a great influence, within the whole field of philosophy and, indeed, even on the most important aims of man in general, the certain and clear insight has into the difference between that which rests on subjective principles of the faculties of the human soul,—both those of the senses and those of the understanding,—and that which goes directly to its objects. Provided one is not carried away by a mania for system-building, the enquiries undertaken into the same basic rule, in its widest application, verify each other. I am thus at the present time occupied working out, in some detail, a book with the title *The Limits of Sensibility and Reason*. It is intended to contain the relation of the fundamental concepts and laws destined for the sensible world, along with an outline of what constitutes the nature of the Doctrine of Taste, Metaphysics and Morals. During the winter I have gone through all the relevant material, examined everything, weighed everything and harmonised everything. But it is only recently that I have completed the plan thereto.

The *second reason* for my silence must be still more valid to you as a physician: namely, that my health has perceptibly suffered. It is thus absolutely necessary to assist my x 118 nature to a gradual recovery and for its sake to avoid all exertions for a time, only using the moments of good spirits and devoting the rest of my time to leisure and small delights. According to my acquaintances, this regimen and the daily use of quinine have already visibly restored me since last October. I am sure that you will not entirely disapprove of a negligence agreeing with pharmaceutical principles.

I have learned with pleasure that you are about to give to the press a treatise on the nature of speculative knowledge.[24] I look forward to it with eagerness, and since it will be ready before my book, I shall still be able to take advantage of all kinds of hints doubtless to be found there. The pleasure that I shall feel at the applause your first publication will presumably receive, although it may secretly have no small content of vanity, will yet really have a strong flavour of unselfish and friendly sympathy. Herr *Kanter* has dispatched my dissertation abroad rather late and in small numbers, without even incorporating such works in the Leipzig Book Fair Catalogue; I was not inclined to alter it in any way, having formed the plan of treating its subject more completely later. Since this is the text about which further will be said in my next book, and since also many separate ideas occur there which I may have difficulty finding an opportunity of introducing, and since the dissertation, with its mistakes, seems not to be worthy of a new imprint, it disappoints me somewhat that this work must so quickly suffer the fate of all human endeavours, namely oblivion.

If you could bring yourself to write, even though you only rarely receive replies, your most extensive letter will perhaps assist my quinine to a spring cure. I beg to make my excuses and to give my assurances of my greatest indebtedness to Herr *Mendelssohn* and to Herr *Lambert*. I think that when my stomach gradually comes to perform its duty, my fingers will not delay to perform theirs. I accompany all your undertakings with the wishes of a sincerely sympathetic friend,

I. Kant.

Königsberg, 7 June 1771.

Letter 5 (LXV)   *21 February 1772*

To MARCUS HERZ

Noble Sir,
Worthy Friend

If you are annoyed at my complete failure to answer your   x 123
letters, you do me indeed no injustice. But, if you draw un-
pleasant inferences from my silence, I would wish to be able
to appeal to your own knowledge of my character. Instead   x 124
of any excuses, I shall briefly relate to you the way in which
my thoughts have been occupied and thereby explain the
deferment of my correspondence in my leisure hours. After
your departure from Königsberg I once more examined in
the intervals—so necessary to me—between business and
relaxation, the project of the observations about which we
had disputed. My intention was to harmonise this project
with the whole of philosophy and the rest of knowledge, and
to grasp its extent and limits. In distinguishing the sensible
from the intellectual in ethics and in the fundamental principles springing from this distinction, I had already made
quite considerable progress in the matter. I had also already
long ago sketched to my moderate satisfaction the principles of feeling, taste and judgement, together with their
effects: the pleasant, the beautiful and the good. I now proposed to myself the project of a work which could be
entitled: *The Limits of Sensibility and Reason.* I conceived it as
having two parts, a theoretical and a practical, the first part
containing in two sections, 1. Phenomenology in general
and 2. Metaphysics according to its nature and method; the
second part containing also two sections: 1. General principles of feeling, taste and the sensible desires. 2. The first
grounds of morality. While I was thinking out the full extent of the theoretical part and the reciprocal relations of its
sections, I noticed that I was still lacking something essential which I, like others, had left out of consideration in my
metaphysical enquiries, and which constituted, indeed, the
key to the whole secret, the key to metaphysics which until

then, had remained hidden to itself. I asked myself namely: on what basis rests the relation to the object of that which, in ourselves, we call representation? If the representation contains merely the way in which the subject is affected by the object, it is easy to understand how it corresponds to the object, as effect to cause, and how this determination of our mind can represent something, i.e. how it can have an object. The passive or sensible representations have therefore an understandable relation to objects; and the principles, derived from the nature of our soul, have an intelligible validity for all things, insofar as they are supposed to be objects of the senses. Similarly, if that in us, which is called representation, were active with respect to the object, i.e. if the object itself were produced by it, in the same way as divine knowledge is imagined as the prototype of things, the conformity of the representation to its object would be intelligible. The possibility, then, both of the archetypal intellect (*intellectus archetypus*) whose intuition is itself the ground of things, and of the derivative intellect (*intellectus ectypus*) which derives from sensible perfection the data for its logical treatment of things, is understandable at least. But our understanding is not, by its representations, the cause of the object (except in the case of good intentions in ethics) nor is the object the cause of the representations of the understanding in the real sense (*in sensu reali*). The pure concepts of the understanding may not, therefore, be abstracted from the perceptions of the senses, nor may the sensitivity of the representations have expression through the senses, but must indeed have their source in the nature of the soul, though not in the sense that it is either caused by the object, or itself productive of the object. I was satisfied in the dissertation to express the nature of the intellectual representations in purely negative terms: namely that they were not modifications of the soul produced by the object. The problem, however, which I passed over in silence, is how, then, a representation which is related to an object can otherwise possibly exist, without being affected by it in some way. I had said: the sensible representations represent things as they appear; the intellectual representations represent them as they are. But by what means are these things given to us, if it is not by the way they affect us; and if such intellectual representations rest on our inner activity, whence comes the agreement which they are supposed to have with objects, the objects not being originated by this activity; and whence is it that the axioms of pure reason concerning these objects agree with them, without this agreement being permitted to derive assistance from experience. This is relevant in mathematics, since the objects before us are only magnitudes and can only be represented as magnitudes, because we can produce their representations when we take one thing several times. Hence, the concepts of magnitude are self-active and their fundamental principles can be constituted a priori. But with regard to qualities the question is, how is the understanding to con- x 126 struct for itself entirely a priori concepts of things, with which the things are necessarily in agreement; how is the understanding to draw up real fundamental principles about their possibility, with which experience is necessarily in faithful agreement, and yet are independent of it;—this question always leaves behind an obscurity with respect to the faculty of our understanding: whence comes the agreement with things.

Plato accepted a past spiritual intuition of Divinity as the original source of the pure concepts of the understanding and of its fundamental principles. *Malebranche*[25] accepted a more permanent, continuous intuition of this Original Being. Various moralists have accepted just this with regard to the ultimate laws of morality. *Crusius*[26] accepted certain innate rules of judgement and certain concepts, as planted by God in the human soul so as to harmonise with things. The former of these systems could be called the Theory of Hyperphysical Influx; the latter, the Theory of Pre-established Intellectual Harmony.[27] But in determining the origin and validity of our knowledge, however, the *deus ex machina* is the most absurd argument one could choose. Apart from the vicious circle in the series of inferences from what we know, the argument has the further disadvantage of countenancing every whim and pious or speculative figment of the imagination.

While I was thus looking for the sources of intellectual knowledge, without which it is impossible to determine the nature and limits of metaphysics, I reduced this science to essentially different sections. I tried to reduce transcendental philosophy, namely all the concepts of completely pure reason, to a certain number of categories, but not in the way *Aristotle* did it. He placed them in his ten predicaments next to each other, merely approximately, as he found them. On the contrary, I tried to make the reduction in accordance with the way in which, by means of a few fundamental laws of the understanding, they divide themselves into classes. I shall not here go into a detailed explanation of the entire succession of enquiries, up to the final end. I can, however, say that, as far as the essential part of my intention is concerned, I have been successful. I am now in the position to present a critique of pure reason, containing the nature both of theoretical, as well as of practical knowledge, insofar as it is purely intellectual. I will first of all elaborate the first part containing the sources of metaphysics, its x 127 method and limits; after that, I will work out the pure principles of morality. As far as the first part is concerned, I shall publish within about three months.

In a mental occupation of such a delicate kind as this, nothing is a greater hindrance than being busily occupied with reflections lying outside the field of enquiry. In quiet or even happy moments the mind must be at all times without interruption open, but not strained, to the reception of any accidental remark that may offer itself. Encouragements and diversions must maintain the strength of the mind in resilience and nimbleness. Thus is one placed in the position to see the object at all times from different directions, and to extend one's range of vision from microscopic observation to a general view, so that one adopts all conceivable standpoints, each of which reciprocally verifies the optical judgement of the other. No other cause than this, my worthy friend, has held back my replies to your so pleasing letters. You did not seem to require that I write empty replies.

With regard to your little work, written with taste and deep reflection: it exceeded my expectation in many parts. But I cannot dilate upon it in detail for the reasons already mentioned. I will, however, say this much, my friend. The effect which undertakings of this kind, with regard to the state of the various branches of knowledge, has among the learned public, is such that these works would just as well be lost to the general benefit, whether they were published or were to remain for ever unknown. I often comfort myself with reflections of this kind, when I begin to worry about the largely completed plan of the most important, in my opinion, of my works, because indispositions threaten to interrupt its execution. For, to induce readers to take the trouble to reflect on one's writings, a writer of more distinction and eloquence is necessary.

I have found reviews of your book in the *Breslauische Zeitung*[28] and quite recently in the *Göttingische Zeitung*.[12] If x 128 the general public judges the spirit and chief intention of a book like this, then all effort is lost. If the reviewer has taken the trouble to see what the essentials of the effort were, even blame is more pleasing to the author than praise arising from a superficial evaluation. The Göttingen reviewer dwells on certain non-essential applications of the system, with respect to which I have myself made some alteration, but only because this contributed something still further to the chief intention. A letter from *Mendelssohn* or *Lambert* is more effective in bringing the author back to the examination of his doctrines, than ten such lightly written assessments. The good pastor *Schulz*,[29] the best philosophic mind that I know in this region, has understood the intention of the system well. I hope he may occupy himself with your little work as well. In his judgement there are two misconceived interpretations of the system, lying before him. The first is that space may perhaps be a true intellectual intuition, and thus something objective, rather than the pure form of sensible appearance. The obvious answer is: for this very reason, space is declared not to be objective and therefore not intellectual either; for, when we completely analyse its representation, we conceive in it neither a representation of things (since they can only exist in space), nor a real connection (which cannot occur in the absence of things); namely, not an effect, nor relations as grounds; and consequently we have no representation at all of a thing, nor of something real inhering in the things. Therefore we conclude that space is nothing objective. The second misunderstanding brings him to an objection that has drawn me into considerable reflection, for it seems to be the most essential objection which can be raised against the system, and which will naturally occur to everyone, and which Herr *Lambert* made against me.[30] The objection is as follows: changes are real (according to the evidence of the inner sense); now they are only possible under the assumption of time. Thus, time is something real, attached to the determinations of things in themselves. Why (I said to myself) does one not reason in accordance with this argument as follows:—bodies are real (according to the evidence of the external senses); now bodies are only possible on the presupposition of space; thus space is something objective x 129 and real inherent in things themselves. The reason is this: since one probably notices that with respect to external things one cannot infer from the reality of representations to the reality of objects; but, with respect to the inner sense, thought or the existence of thoughts is one and the same with myself. Herein lies the key to this difficulty: there is no doubt that I ought not to think of my own state under the form of time, and that, therefore, the form of inner sensibility does not give me the appearance of change. Now, that change is something real, I deny as little as that bodies are something real, although I simply understand by that merely that something real corresponds to the appearance. I cannot even say: the inner appearance changes, for by what means would I observe this change, if it did not appear to my inner sense. Should anyone wish to assert that it follows from this that everything in the world is objective and in itself unchangeable, I would reply: they are neither changeable nor unchangeable, as *Baumgarten*[31] says in paragraph 18 of his *Metaphysica*:[32] 'What is absolutely impossible is neither hypothetically possible nor impossible, for it cannot be regarded under any condition at all'. Similarly: the things of the world are, objectively or in themselves, neither in one and the same state at different times nor in a different state; for, in this sense, they are not represented at all in time. But enough of this. It seems that one finds no hearing with merely negative propositions. One must construct something in the place of that which one has destroyed; or at least, when one has disposed of the chimaera, one must make the pure insight of the understanding dogmatically intelligible and indicate its limits. I am occupied with this task, and this is the reason why, often against my intention, I withhold the leisure hours allowed me by my very changing constitution for reflection from the answering of friendly letters, but surrender myself to the natural tendency of my thoughts. Surrender, then, your right over me of retaliation by withholding from me your letters because you find me so negligent in replying. Just as I reckon with your continuous affection and friendship towards me, so can you always retain mine with reassurance. Should you be satisfied with short replies, you will not lack them in the future. The assurance of honest sympathy must take x 130 the place of formalities between us. As a sign of your sincere reconciliation I await a pleasant letter from you in the immediate future. Fill it with news, which will not be lacking to you, being as you are in the seat of learning; and pardon the freedom with which I make this request. Greet Herr *Mendelssohn* and Herr *Lambert* from me, and Herr *Sulzer* as well, and present any apologies with similar reasons to those I have given you. Be always my friend as I am yours,

I. Kant.

Königsberg, 21 February 1772.

Letter 6 (LXXI)   *Towards the end 1773*

To MARCUS HERZ

x 136   Noble Sir,

Most worthy friend,

I am pleased to receive news of the good progress of your efforts, and I am still more pleased to see the tokens of your kind remembrance and friendship in the letter you sent me. The exercise in the practical side of pharmaceutics, under the guidance of an adept teacher, is certainly in accordance with my wish. The churchyard must not in the future be filled until the young doctor learns the method of rightly tackling the practical side. Make plenty of observations. Theories are here, as elsewhere, more often concerned with conceptual clarification than with the disclosure of natural phenomena. *Macbride's*[33] systematic pharmaceutics (I think it will already be familiar to you) pleased me very well in this respect. I feel much better on the whole now than I did before; the reason being that I now know better what does not suit me. Because of my sensitive nerves medicine is, without exception, poison for me. The only medicine that I use, and that only rarely, if acidity troubles me in the morning, is half a teaspoonful of quinine with water. I find this much better than any absorbents. Apart from this, I have given up the daily use of this medicinal, in the intention of toughening myself. This very medicine produced an intermittent pulse, especially towards evening. This made me rather worried until I suspected the reason, and, having given it up, the complaint ceased immediately.

x 137   Do study the great variety of natures. Every surgeon who was not a philosopher would throw mine to the winds.

118

You seek industriously but unsuccessfully in the Leipzig Book Fair Catalogue for a certain name under the letter K. After the great effort I have taken, nothing would have been easier for me than to have paraded my name there with not inconsiderable works which I have almost completed. But since I have come so far in my intention of remodelling a branch of learning so long worked in vain by half the philosophical world that I now find myself in possession of a system that completely solves the hitherto unsolved riddle and brings the procedure of self-isolating reason under sure and easily applicable rules, I am now sticking stubbornly to my intention of not allowing myself to be led astray by vanity of authorship into seeking fame in an easier and better liked field, before I have levelled my thorny and hard plot and freed it for general cultivation.

I don't think that there are many who have tried to outline a completely new branch of learning in accordance with a previously worked out idea, and have at the same time tried to execute it completely. With regard to the method of arranging the exactly denominated parts into classes: you can scarcely imagine the trouble this causes and how much time has to be devoted to it. But in return, a ray of hope shines towards me, a hope which I could not reveal to anyone other than you, without the fear of being suspected of the most extreme vanity: the hope, namely, of giving to philosophy, by this means, a new and lasting turn of far greater advantage to religion and morals, and also of giving to philosophy a form that can tempt the reserved mathematician into regarding philosophy as capable and worthy of his study. I still occasionally entertain the hope of delivering the completed work by Easter. However, when I reckon with the frequent indispositions which are continually interrupting my work, I can promise it, notwithstanding, almost certainly a short time after Easter.

I am eager to see the appearance of your effort in moral philosophy. But I would nonetheless have wished that you had not wanted to validate there the concept of reality, a x 138 concept so important in the highest abstraction of speculative reason, and yet so empty when applied to the practical. For the concept is transcendental; but the highest practical elements are desire and aversion and these are empirical, no matter from whence their object is recognised. An entirely pure concept of the understanding cannot give laws or prescriptions to what is only sensible, for a pure concept is quite unconditioned with respect to the sensible. The highest ground of morality must not merely allow one to make an inference to pleasure; it must itself please in the highest degree, for it is not merely a speculative representation; it must also have motive power and therefore, although it is indeed intellectual, it must still have a direct relation to the first motives of the will. I shall be pleased when I have completed my transcendental philosophy, which is really a critique of pure reason. Thereupon I shall go on to the metaphysics which has only two parts: the metaphysics of nature and the metaphysics of morals. I will publish the latter of these two parts first. I look forward in advance to the publication of this work.

I have read the review of *Platner's Anthropology*.[34] It is certainly true that I would not have guessed at the reviewer, but the progress of his skill, which he reveals, pleases me. This winter I am holding for a second time a private seminar on anthropology, a subject which I am now thinking of getting officially recognised as an academic discipline. My intention however is quite different: my intention is to reveal the sources of all knowledge, those of morals, of skill, of intercourse, of the method of educating and ruling man, and consequently of everything practical. After that, I seek further the phenomena and their laws, as the first grounds of the possibility of the modification of human nature in general. Thus, that subtle enquiry—doomed in my eyes for ever to failure—that subtle enquiry into the manner in which bodily organs are related to thoughts is omitted. I am unremittingly so taken up with observations myself in ordinary life that from start to finish my audience is never bored but rather entertained, because of the continually offered opportunity of comparing their common experience with my remarks. In between times I try to make out of this,   x 139 in my opinion, very pleasant, empirical enquiry a preliminary exercise for the academic youth in skill, cleverness and even wisdom. This subject, together with physical geography, differs from all other instructions and can be called knowledge of the world.

I have seen my portrait in front of the library. It is an honour which disturbs me a little because, as you know, I very much try to avoid all appearance of surreptitious praise and importuning for the sake of creating an impression. It is well painted, although it is not a good likeness. However, I learn with pleasure that such is the product of the lovable party-feeling of my past students. The review of your book, occurring in the same piece, proves what I feared: that in order to place new thoughts in such a light that the reader perceives the real intention of the author and the weight of his arguments, a somewhat lengthier period of time is necessary in order to think oneself into the position of a complete and facile acquaintance.

I am, with most sincere friendship and respect,
Your most devoted servant and friend,
I. Kant.

Letter 7 (CI)

24 November 1776

To MARCUS HERZ

Noble Dr.

x 184

Most worthy friend,

I am very pleased to have received through Herr *Friedländer*[35] news of your good progress in medical practice. Apart from the advantage it creates, this is a field where the understanding receives continual nourishment from new insights, since it is maintained in moderate activity, without being worn out by use. This is the experience of our greatest analysts, the experience of a *Baumgarten, Mendelssohn, Garve,*[36] whom I follow from a distance. They spin out their brain nerves into the finest threads and thus make themselves extremely sensitive to every impression or tension in them. With them this may be merely a play of thoughts for relaxation, but never a tiring occupation.

It was with pleasure that I observed the purity of expression, the pleasantness of the style and the subtlety of the remarks in your book on the difference of taste.[37] I am not now in a position to add any particular judgement that occurred to me in reading, for it was lent to me, though I do not know by whom. One passage remains in my memory for which I must rebuke you, on account of your friendly bias towards me. The praise which you give me, along with *Lessing*—disturbs me. For I do not really possess the merit worthy of your praise; and it is as if I saw at the side a mocker, attributing to me pretensions like this, and deriving from them opportunity for ill-intentioned censure.

Indeed, I do not give up hope of merit in the field I am working in. I receive from all sides rebukes on account of the inactivity into which I seem long to have fallen. And yet, nevertheless, I have really not been more systematically and persistently occupied than now, since the years when you last saw me. The material which, if worked out, would bring me, I could perhaps hope, transitory applause, piles up under my hands, as customarily happens, when one becomes possessed of a few fruitful principles. But it is altogether held up by one major object, as by a dam. I hope, by its means, to acquire a permanent merit. This chief object, which I believe myself really already to possess, now necessitates probably not so much being thought out as being merely completed. After I have done this work which I am first beginning now, having overcome the last hindrances only last summer, I will make myself a free field, the cultivation of which will be for me purely entertainment. To carry out such a plan as this with steadiness requires, if I may say so, persistence. I am often incited by the difficul-

ties to apply myself to other more pleasant matters. But it
is in part the overcoming of certain of the difficulties, in
part the importance of the business itself that has intermittently witheld me from such infidelity. You know, it must
be possible to see the field of pure reason independent of
empirical principles in its judgements, since it lies in us *a
priori* and can expect no revelations from experience. Now,
in order to delineate, in accordance with sure principles, the
complete compass, divisions, limits and whole content of
pure reason, and in order to place the boundary-stones so x 186
that one may know with certainty in the future whether one
is on the territory of reason or on that of sophistry, the following is essential: a critique, a discipline, a canon, an
archetectonic of *pure reason*, and consequently a formal
science needing nothing derived from the already existent
branches of knowledge, but requiring for its establishment
even technical expressions, peculiar entirely to itself. I do
not expect to be through with this work before Easter and
I intend to devote part of next summer to this purpose,
assuming that my continually interrupted health permits
me to work. But, with regard to this intention, please do not
raise expectations; they are sometimes wont to be troublesome and often detrimental.

And now, dear friend, please do not retaliate against my
negligence in letter writing, but rather honour me, from
time to time, with news, in particular, literary news of your
area. Present my most devoted respects to Herr *Mendelssohn* and likewise to Herr *Engel* and *Lambert*, as opportunity offers; and to Herr *Bode* too, who greeted me through
Dr. *Reccard*. And please retain in constant friendship.

Your most devoted servant
and friend,
I. Kant.

Königsberg, 24 November 1776.

Letter 8 (CXXI)   *April 1778*

To MARCUS HERZ

x 214 Choice and inestimable friend,

Letters such as I receive from you place me in a state of feeling which, according to my taste, deeply sweetens my life and which seems, to a certain extent, to be a foretaste of another life, when I think I read in your honest and thankful soul the comforting proof of a not entirely disappointed hope, that my academic life will not slip by quite fruitlessly, as far as its chief aim is concerned, which I have constantly before my eyes; the aim, namely, of spreading good mental attitudes, based on maxims, of fixing them in well dispositioned souls, and, by this means, of giving the only purposeful direction to the cultivation of the talents.

In this connection, the pleasant feeling is mixed, after all, with something of melancholy, when I see opened before me a scene where this intention could be promoted in a far wider domain, and yet, at the same time, find myself excluded by the small share of vitality allotted me. As you know, profit and fame on a great stage have little attraction for me. All that I have wished and received is a peaceful situation, exactly suited to my needs, and a variable occupation of work, speculation and social intercourse, where my spirit, easily affected but otherwise free from cares, and where my body, still more capricious, but never actually ill, can be kept occupied without becoming exhausted. All change makes me anxious, although it may give the strongest impression of improving my condition. And I think I must respect this instinct of my nature, if I am to draw out still further the thread which the *Parcae* have spun so thin and delicate. The greatest thanks then to my patrons and friends who are so amicably disposed towards me as to take my well being to heart. But at the same time I have a most humble request: that you devote this amicable disposition to protecting me in my present state from all disturbance—

from which, indeed, I have been always free—and to take me into your protection.

Your medical prescriptions, dear friend, are very welcome to me, in case of necessity. But since your prescriptions contain laxatives which seriously assail my con- x 215 stitution and are inevitably succeeded by intensified constipation, and since, so long as evacuation occurs regularly each morning, I really am healthy in my own fashion i.e. in a weakly sort of way, and since also I have never enjoyed much better health than now, I am determined to surrender myself further to the care of nature and only to resort to artificial measures, when it denies its support.

The report that some sheets of my present work are supposed already to be printed is prematurely divulged. Since I do not wish that anything should be forced from me (for I would still like to work longer in the world) many other works cross each other. It makes progress however and I hope it will be ready this summer. You will allow, some day, I hope, that the causes of the delay in the appearance of a work, not amounting to much in terms of pages, are validly grounded in the nature of the matter and of the project itself. *Tetens*,[38] in his extensive work on human nature, has a great deal to say that is penetrating. But there is no doubt that he published it exactly as he wrote it; or at least left it uncorrected. It seems to me that, when he wrote his long enquiry into freedom in the second volume, he was hoping all the time to find his way safely out of this labyrinth by means of a few ideas which he had drawn up for himself in uncertain outlines. Having tired both himself and his reader, the matter remained in the end as he had found it and he advises the reader to consult his own feelings.

Should I pass this summer in tolerable health, I think I shall be able to communicate the promised work to the public.

While writing this, I have received another gracious letter from His Excellency, Herr *von Zedlitz*, the Minister of State,[39] with the repeated offer of a chair in Halle, which I must nevertheless beg leave to decline, for the insuperable reasons already mentioned.

Since I must immediately answer *Breitkopf*[40] in Leipzig on his suggestion that I develop more extensively for him the material on the races of mankind, the present letter must wait for the next post.

x 216 Do give my most friendly greetings to Herr *Mendelssohn*, and express my wish that he may enjoy in increasing health his naturally cheerful heart and the amusements which his goodness and his always fruitful spirit may obtain for him.

Retain in affection and friendship
Your always devoted, true servant
I. Kant.

P.S. I ask most devotedly that the enclosed letter should be given to the post, if necessary with the required postage etc.

Letter 9 (CXXVII)   *August 1778*

To MARCUS HERZ

x 224 Most worthy friend,

It cannot be other than very pleasant for me to comply with your request, especially since the intention is one that stands in relation to my own interest.[41] But it is impossible to satisfy your wish as quickly as you ask. Everything dependent on the diligence and cleverness of my students is precarious, since it is a piece of good fortune to have within a given time span attentive and capable hearers, and those that one had a short while ago are scattered and cannot easily be found again. One can rarely persuade someone to give away his own transcript. But I shall see about effecting this as soon as possible. I may be able to find something detailed here or there on logic. But metaphysics is a course which I have so worked at during the latter years that I am afraid it may be difficult, even for a sharp intellect, to make out from the transcription what the precise idea was, even though it was, in my opinion, intelligible in the lecture. But, since the notion has been apprehended by a beginner, and since it deviates considerably both from my earlier concepts and from those that are generally accepted, I fear it would require a mind as good as yours to represent it systematically and intelligibly.

I am still working tirelessly on my handbook on this part of philosophy; when I have it ready, which will, I think, be quite soon now, every transcription of it will be perfectly intelligible on account of the clearness of the plan. I will, however, take the trouble, as far as is possible, to find out a transcription serviceable for your purposes. Herr *Kraus*[42] has been now some weeks in Elbing, but he will soon be returning and I will talk to him about this matter. Anyway, start on the logic, and while you are still occupied with that, the material for the remainder will already have been collected. Although this is supposed to be an occupation for the winter, the supply of material can be gathered together before the passing of the summer, and thus give you time for preparation. Herr *Joel*[43] says that he left me in health. And it is true, I am well, having accustomed myself for many years now to regard a very limited well being, which the majority of people would greatly complain about, as health; x 225 and having accustomed myself to cheer myself up as far as possible, to take good care of myself and to make a recovery. Without this hindrance, my little projects, at which I have otherwise enjoyed working, would, I think, long have reached completion. I am with unchangeable friendship and affection,

Your most devoted,
I. Kant.

Königsberg, 28 August 1778.

P.S. Did you receive the letter I despatched to you
    about six months ago, together with an enclosure for
    Breitkopf in Leipzig?

Letter 10 (CXXXI)   *December 1778*

To MARCUS HERZ

x 228   Most worthy friend,

I have not been unmindful of your commission, although I could not carry it out immediately. It was scarcely possible for me to get hold of a transcript of a lecture course of the philosophical encyclopaedia; and then I did not have the time to read it through or alter anything in it. Nevertheless I am sending it to you, since it may perhaps be possible to find something in it, or to infer something from it, which could make more easily intelligible a systematic concept of the pure knowledge of the understanding, insofar as such knowledge takes its origin from a principle in us. Herr *Kraus*, to whom I have also given this, has promised to find on his journey one or, maybe, two transcripts of the course on metaphysics and to give them to you. After starting coming to my classes he has since applied himself to other subjects. For this reason he will not occupy himself with your lectures at all. And I find this the most advisable too, for such lectures in matters of this kind would only open up a theatre of disputes.

I most earnestly recommend him to your friendship, as a
x 229   well thinking and promising young man. The reason why I have not been lucky in procuring detailed transcripts is this: since 1770 I have only lectured publicly on Logic and Metaphysics and know very few of my hearers. They also soon disperse, so that one cannot trace them again. All the same, I had hoped to be able to procure for you the Prologemena of Metaphysics, in particular, and the Ontology, as they are treated in my new course of lectures. There, the nature of this knowledge or subtilising is far better analysed than elsewhere. And a great deal has been introduced, on the publication of which I am working.

By the time this letter reaches you, Herr *Kraus* will already perhaps have arrived, or will arrive between this post and the next. It is with the next post that I shall write to the Minister, Herr *von Zedlitz* and his secretary; of the latter, namely Herr *Biester*,[44] I request that, in case Herr *Kraus* should arrive before my letter, you most kindly anticipate him, and ask him to deliver the manuscript on physical geography which he is bringing with him to His Excellency.

I close now hastily in the hope of being able to converse more with you in the immediate future, and with the sentiment of a sincerely devoted friend,

and servant
I. Kant.

Königsberg,
15th December 1778.

Letter 11 (CXXXII)   *January 1779*

To MARCUS HERZ

Noble Sir,   x 230
Most worthy friend,
I have received your present of the plaster cast of Herr *Mendelssohn's* medallion through a pleasant young gentleman, Herr *von Nolten*. I thank you most devotedly for it.

Dr. *Heintz*[45] assures me from the letters of Herr Secretary *Biester* that your lectures are received with general and unusual approbation. Herr *Kraus* now reports to me exactly the same and informs me of the universal respect which you have won among the Berlin public. I do not need to assure you that this awakens in me exceptional joy. That much is self-evident. But what surprises me here is not so much your aptitude and insight, in which I have every reason to place my complete trust in any case, so much as the popularity with regard to which I would have been quite anxious in any undertaking of this kind. For some time in certain leisure hours I have been reflecting on the principles of popularity in the various departments of knowledge in general (obviously in such as I am capable of, for mathematics is not one of them), particularly in philosophy; and from this point of view, I think I can determine not merely a different selection, but also quite a different arrangement from that demanded by the scholastic rule, although this remains the foundation. However, your success shows that you have not failed in this matter, and straight away at your first attempt.

How much I wish I could be of service to you with something better than the manuscript which Herr *Kraus* will hand to you. Had I been able last winter to foresee this, I would have made some arrangement with my students. It will be wretchedly little that you will be able to find out from these meagre papers, and yet your genius will be able to make it develop luxuriantly. If they are of no further use to you, Herr *Toussaint*, who is now in Berlin, will request them of you, so as to bring them back shortly before Easter.

Could your influence be of some use to Herr *Kraus*, which I do not doubt, I request you most earnestly to exercise it. I count on it as an effect of the friendship with which you honour me, and in respect of which you have never left me the least doubt. He is a modest and grateful young man who promises great things. He will neither discredit nor be insensible of your recommendation, should you be willing for his sake to recommend him to the Minister, as you have the opportunity. Nothing stands in his way apart from certain hypochondriac cares, with which such young thinking minds as his torment themselves, often without cause. Your art doubtless contains antidotes to this weakness, and your friendship still greater ones, should you be willing to honour him with it. I receive all news, direct or indirect, of your growing good fortune with new pleasure, and I am in eternal friendship

x 231

> Your devoted and true servant
> I. Kant.

V

Selections from Kant's correspondence with Beck (1791-3)

Letter 12 (CDXXXVIII)   *9 May 1791*

To JACOB SIGISMUND BECK[1]

Noble Magister,   XI 243
Very highly esteemed friend,
It was very pleasant for me to receive the news of your
entering your new career,[2] namely, that of an academic
teacher, along with the present of your dissertation, which is
ample proof of the great aptitude necessary for such a
career. I was at the same time reminded of a sin of omission,
which can be made good again, I hope.

I had, namely, when you were in Halle for the first time,
recommended you, as the opportunity offered, to the Chan-
cellor, Herr *von Hoffmann*, with whom I was by chance in
correspondence. But I learned afterwards that you had
postponed your original intention of taking the Doctor's
degree and had returned to Prussia for a year. When I
afterwards heard that you were in Halle a second time, I
wrote again to Herr *von Hoffmann*, so that he might contribute to the furtherance of your academic progress, a thing
which lay within his power. This very worthy man replied:
'*I have met Magister Beck on returning from my Swiss journey.
I shall be delighted to be of use to him.*' He added that he was
willing to use his influence on behalf of a deserving person,
even though, having been, in accordance with his repeatedly   XI 244
expressed wish, relieved of the Chancellorship, his word
could have little weight either with his university colleagues
or with the University of Halle itself, of which he said that
its interest would remain at all times imprinted in his heart,
and that he would always endeavour to be of use to it.

Now, it would have been necessary to inform you of this so that you might have written yourself sometime to Herr *von Hoffmann* (Privy Counsellor) and have suggested something which could have been useful to you. But whether I assumed you would do it of your own accord or whether I intended to inform you of my recommendation and then forgot, I have in any case failed to let you know.

My opinion was, namely, that since the subsistence based on the mere holding of seminars is always very precarious,[3] you would wish like other teachers in your position to seek a post in a school or something similar. This would certainly have furnished your requirements. The influence of Privy Counsellor *von Hoffmann* would doubtless have been of assistance. If this worthy man can be of help to you in this or some similar matter apply to him without hesitation, mentioning my name.

I see from the theses appended to your dissertation that you have understood my concepts far more correctly than many others who otherwise applaud me. With the exactitude and clearness which you, as a mathematician, are able to give your lectures even in the field of metaphysics, the Critique would, I suspect, give you material for a course which would attract a greater number of students than is, unfortunately, common with mathematics lectures.—Please give my regards to Prof. *Jacob*,[4] and convey my thanks to him for his prize essay, which he sent me last year. I am afraid that I have not yet answered the letter that was attached. I am hoping to do so in the immediate future. I ask that the worthy young man may be willing to indulge my 68th year, begun last month. I recently heard from Dr *Conradi*, staff physician, a close friend of Prof. *Jacob*, that the latter has received an invitation to the university of Giessen. I am beginning now to have my doubts about this. When you have any spare time give me good news both about what concerns the above matter and about the latest literary developments. But let it be well understood: I should regard it as an insult if you were to frank your letter.

XI 245

Please assure Prof. *Klügel*[5] of my esteem when you have the opportunity, and be furthermore assured that I am, at all times, with respect and friendship,

> Noble Sir,
> Your most devoted servant,
> I. Kant.

Königsberg, 9 May 1791.

Letter 13 (CDLVII)   *Königsberg 27 Sept. 1791*

To JACOB SIGISMUND BECK

You will perceive, most worthy friend, from the enclosed XI 277
letter of *Hartknoch's*[6] to myself, that he wants someone competent, who is both willing and able to make a synthetic extract from my critical writings, composed in his own manner and with the originality of his own way of thinking. After the revelation made in your last letter of your inclination to occupy yourself with this study, I was unable to suggest anyone more capable or more reliable than yourself. I have therefore suggested you to him. I have myself something to gain in making this suggestion, of course. But I am, at the same time, certain that if you are able to convince yourself of the real importance of that adaptation, once started on it, you will find yourself an inexhaustible supply of entertainment for reflection in those intervals when you rest from mathematics—which you must not by any means prejudice with this work—and conversely, when you tire of the former, you will be able to find a desired refreshment in mathematics. For partly my own experience and partly—to a far greater extent—the example of the greatest mathematicians convince me that mathematics cannot by itself afford satisfaction to the soul of a thinking man. I am convinced that something else, even if it be merely poetry, as with *Kästner*,[7] is necessary; something else which partly refreshes the spirit by merely occupying its other natural capacities, and which partly affords the spirit an

alternating nourishment. What could be more appropriate to this end—and that for the whole period of one's life—than amusing oneself with what concerns the destiny of

xi 278 man: especially when one entertains the hope of systematically thinking it out, and now and again of making some financial profit. Besides, the history of learning and the world in general are lastly agreed in this. Nor have I entirely given up the hope that, even if this study cannot throw any new light on mathematics, the reverse may yet be the case; that, in reflecting on its methods and heuristic principles, together with reflection on the needs and desiderata still attached to it, mathematics could reach new discoveries for the critique and measuring out of pure reason; and that this new method of representing their abstract concepts would provide something similar to *Leibniz's 'ars univeralis characteristica combinatoria'*. For both the tables of categories as well as those of ideas (among which the cosmological show an intrinsic similarity to impossible roots)* have after all been counted. And as far as every possible use of reason is concerned, they have been determined in as great detail as mathematics could require for the purpose of seeking how much clarity, if not enlargement, can be introduced by their means.

Now, as far as Herr *Hartknock's* suggestion is concerned, I gather from your letter communicated by him, that you do not absolutely turn down his proposal. I think it would be a good idea if you were to start work on it straightaway, first of all in order to draw up a rough outline of the system; or, should you already have thought of this, to seek out those parts of the system which may perhaps cause you difficulty and to communicate your doubts and difficulties to me from time to time; (in which case I would be glad if someone, perhaps Prof. *Jacob*—and please greet him heartily from me—were to be of assistance to you in looking up in

---

* If according to the principle 'everything is conditioned in the series of appearances', I were to strive for the unconditioned and ultimate ground of the whole series, it would be as if I were seeking $\sqrt{-2}$.

all the polemical writings the terminological contradictions alleged against me, for example in the essays and particularly in the reviews in *Eberhard's Magazine*,[8] early articles in the *Tübinger gelehrte Zeitung*[9] and anywhere else where suchlike may be found. For I have found it so easy to untangle the misunderstanding in these objections that I would have long ago drawn them up in a collection and refuted them, had I not forgotten to note them down and XI 279 collect them together as I came across them). We can still think about a Latin translation, when your work has been published in German.

With regard to the two treatises proposed to *Hartknoch*, namely that on *Reinhold's*[10] theory of the representative faculty and that comparing *Hume's* and *Kant's* philosophy (respecting the latter treatise, please examine the volume of his essays where his moral principle is to be found, so as to compare it with my own. His aesthetic principle is to be found there as well.)—with regard, then, to these two treatises: should the latter not take up too much of your time, it would naturally be preferable, for the time being, to working at the former subject. For *Reinhold*, an otherwise dear person, has so passionately entered into his own theory, which is not entirely intelligible to myself, that should it happen that in one or other of his pieces, or even perhaps with regard to his whole thought, you were not agreed with him, he would become dissatisfied with his friends. Nevertheless I really do hope that nothing hinders you from working at and publishing the former examination. I make the suggestion that, when you honour me with your answer to this letter, you may express your opinion as to whether you agree to my writing to *Reinhold* and acquainting him with your character and present occupation, and since you are so near each other, to my establishing a literary correspondence between you both. This would certainly please him very much. Perhaps a friendly agreement could be established about what you wish to write on the subject mentioned above.

I will act as intermediary between you and *Hartknoch*, for the honorarium for your work (both philosophical and mathematical), if you only give me a few hints about it; you do not need to let him have your work for less than five or six Reichsthaler a sheet.

I remain with the greatest respect and most friendly affection,

Your
I. Kant.

Königsberg, 27 September 1791.

P.S. Please, once more, do not on any account spare me the postage.

Letter 14 (CDLXIV)   *2 November 1791*

To JACOB SIGISMUND BECK

xi 290 Most worthy Magister,

My reply to your pleasant letter of 8 October comes somewhat late, but I hope not so late after all as to have held you up in your work. My work as Dean and other business has held me up until now; they even banished from my thoughts my intention of replying.

Your doubts about associating yourself with that troublesome crowd of book publishers, merely for the sake of profit, is quite justified. But just as reasonable is your decision, however, to make your contribution to the public capital of knowledge like your predecessors (whose posthumous funds you have used), without the motive of gain, since you think you are able to lay before the public 'something thoughtful and useful'.

It is true, I would have wished that you had chosen the first of the two treatises suggested by you to Herr *Hart-*
xi 291 *knoch*, in order to make your début; *Reinhold's* theory of the representative faculty deteriorates so much into obscure abstractions that it is impossible to represent what he says by examples; and consequently, even if you were right in

136

all the individual parts, (which I really could not judge, since I have not myself succeeded in entering into his thought), the theory itself, just because of this difficulty, could not possibly have any extensive or permanent effect; and your judgement also, in particular,—even though the example you most kindly sent me had most pleasingly convinced me of your gift for clarity,—would not have been able to avoid the obscurity inherent in the matter itself. Above all, I do not want Herr *Reinhold* to derive the suspicion from your paper that I had encouraged or occasioned you to write it, for it is rather your own choice. Furthermore, I cannot, at least for the time being, introduce you to him as I thought, since it may then easily appear to him as false friendship. Also, I have no doubt that the tone of your writing will not contain anything that is hard or annoying for this good and otherwise intelligent, though now, as it seems to me, somewhat hypochondriac man.

Your plan, most worthy friend, of making an extract from my critical writings, is a very interesting promise for me, since you testify to being convinced of their truth and usefulness. For I think I am no longer obliged to do this myself because of my age; and, of all those who may wish to undertake this business, a mathematician must be the most welcome to me. Please tell me about the difficulties which have arisen in connection with your own ethics. It will be a pleasure to me to try to solve them, and since I have for a long time frequently traversed this field of enquiry in all directions, I hope I will be able to solve your problems.

I am keeping the sample of your treatise since I find no mention in your letter that I should return it.

But I cannot reconcile myself to the fact that at the end of your letter you remark that for this once you have not franked it, according to my wishes; and yet I received it franked. Be so good as not to do this on any account in the future. For me the expense of your correspondence is negligible; but for you at the present time and also for a considerable time to come, the expense is considerable enough for our correspondence to stop from time to time, which would be a loss for me.

XI 292   Prof. *Kraus* wishes to make all those academics into bachelors who talk to each other about not having any more children, because so many die soon after birth. This wish belongs to his firmly settled principles. And of all people there is probably none less in a position to dissuade him than myself. Regarding the side you intend to take in this matter remain at all times completely free, as far as I am concerned. I do not ask to commit a writer's sin and to bear the guilt of the conscientious scruples that may perhaps sometime arise or be caused by others. I remain furthermore, with all esteem and friendship,

> Your most devoted servant,
> I. Kant.

Königsberg,
2 November 1791.

Letter 15 (CDLXVIII)   *20 January 1792*

To JACOB SIGISMUND BECK
XI 300
Most worthy friend,
I have made you wait a long time for a reply to your letter of 9 December of last year; and yet without guilt, for pressing business hung round my neck; age laid upon me a necessity that would not otherwise have been felt: the necessity of not interrupting with alien affairs my reflection on a subject which I am working at, until I have completed it. For otherwise I am unable to find the thread again once I have dropped it. There should not be in the future, as I hope, such a long delay again.

You submitted to me your thorough examination of just the most difficult part of the whole critique, namely the analysis of an experience in general, and the principles of its possibility. I have already planned considering this difficulty in a system of metaphysics: beginning with the categories in order, (having previously explained simply the pure intuitions of space and time, in which alone objects are given to them, without enquiring further into their possibility), I now prove at the conclusion of the exposition of each of these categories, for example of quantity and all the predicates subordinate to it, along with examples of their use,—I now prove that no experience of the objects of the senses is possible, except insofar as I presuppose *a priori* that they have altogether to be thought of as magnitudes; and so with all other objects. Whereby, then, it is always noted that they are only represented as given in space and time. Out of this, then, originates a whole science of ontology i.e. as *immanent* thought of that, the objective reality of whose concepts can be assured. Only afterwards, in the second section, is it shown that all *conditions* of the possi- xi 301 bility of objects are repeatedly *conditioned*; and yet reason unavoidably drives towards the *unconditioned*, where our thought becomes *transcendental*: that is, objective reality cannot at all be procured for its concepts as ideas, and thus no *knowledge* of the objects can occur by its means. In the dialectic of pure reason, (the setting up of its antinomies), I wanted to show that those objects of possible experience, taken as objects of the senses, do not show the objects as things in themselves, but rather only as appearances; that they now make representable, for the first time, the deduction of the categories in relation to the sensible forms of space and time, as conditions of the connection with a possible experience; and that then they constitute the boundary, extended over the limits of the senses but not affording knowledge, to the categories conceived as concepts for thinking of objects in general (the intuition may be of what form it will). But enough of this.

You have expressed it quite well when you say: 'the *essence* of representations is to relate the object of the mind and the action of the mind to the object, whereby the essence of the representations is represented.' One can only add to this: how can an essence, a complex of representations, be represented. Not through the consciousness that it is *given* to us; for an essence requires *composition* (synthesis) of what is multiple. It must therefore, as essence, be *made*, and what is more, by means of an inner action, that passes for a *given* multiplex in general and proceeds *a priori*, in the way in which this is given; that is, it can only be *thought* through the synthetic unity of the consciousness of it in a concept (of the object in general); and this concept, unconditioned with respect to the way something may be given in the intuition, related to object in general, is the category. The merely subjective state of the representing subject, insofar as the multiple in him (for the composition and its synthetic unity) is given in a special fashion, is called sensibility and this kind of intuition, given *a priori*, is called the sensible form of the intuition. In connection with it, objects are *apprehended* by means of the categories merely as things in appearance and not according to what they are in themselves. Without any intuition they would not xi 302 be apprehended at all, but rather thought; and when one does not merely abstract from all intuition but actually excludes it, objective reality cannot be assured to the categories (there is no assurance that they represent anything at all and are not empty concepts).

Perhaps you can avoid initially defining sensibility by receptivity, that is, defining the kind of representations, as they are in the subject, insofar as it is affected by objects. Rather place it in that, which, in knowledge, constitutes merely the relation of the representation to the subject, so that its form reveals, in this relation to the object of the intuition, nothing more than its appearance. But the reason why this subjectivity constitutes merely the way in which the subject is affected by representations, and consequently constitutes their mere receptivity, is already to be found in the fact that it is merely a determination of the subject.

In a word, since this whole analysis simply has the intention of showing by means of certain synthetic principles that experience itself is only possible *a priori*; but since this can only be made rightly intelligible when the principles are really stated, I hold it for advisable to set to work as shortly as possible before these principles are set up. Perhaps the way in which I proceed in my lectures, where I have to be short, can be helpful to you to a certain extent.

I begin by defining experience through empirical *knowledge*. Knowledge is, however, the representation of a *given* object, as of such and such a kind, by means of *concepts*; the knowledge is empirical, when the object is given in the representation of the senses (which contains, therefore, at the same time, sensation and this is connected with consciousness, that is, perception). It is *a priori* knowledge when the object is indeed given but not in the sensible representation (which can nonetheless always be sensible). Two kinds of representation are required for knowledge. 1. intuition, whereby an object is given and 2. concept, whereby it is thought. In order to make a united piece of knowledge out of these two *separate pieces of knowledge* a further action is required: to compound the multiplex given in the intuition, in accordance with the synthetic unity of the consciousness expressed by the concept. Now, since composition through the object or its representation in intuition is *not given*, but can only be *made*, it rests on the pure xi 303 spontaneity of the understanding in concepts of objects in general (on the composition of the multiple datum). But since concepts too, to which no corresponding object can be given at all and which are therefore without any object, would not even be concepts (thoughts whereby I think nothing at all), a multiplex, just as *a priori*, must be given *a priori* for those concepts. And furthermore since it is given *a priori* it must be given in an intuition without a thing as an object; i.e. in the mere form of intuition which is merely subjective (space and time); it must consequently be given, conformable to the merely sensible intuition, whose synthesis is made by means of the imagination, under the rule of the synthetic unity of the consciousness, contained in the concept. Since, then, the rule is concerned with perceptions (in which things are given to the senses through sensation), it is the rule of the schematism of the concepts of the understanding.

I close, herewith, my hastily composed plan and I ask that you do not allow yourself to hold back from revealing your thoughts to me whenever difficulty arises because of my delay in replying to you, a delay caused by accidental hindrances. I am, with highest respect,

Your
I. Kant.

Königsberg, 20 January 1792.
P.S. Do please give the accompanying letter to the post immediately.

Letter 16 (CDLXXXVIII)   *3 July 1792*

To JACOB SIGISMUND BECK

xi 333   Highly esteemed friend,

It is quite certainly not disregard for the question you proposed to me which has hindered me from answering your letter, but rather other work which I had then ventured on. And my age necessitates my not interrupting with anything irrelevant my reflection on a matter with which I am occupied, for otherwise I cannot find the thread again after I have dropped it.—The difference between the connection of the representations in a concept and that in a judgement, for example, 'the dark man' and 'the man is dark' (in other words: 'the man who is dark' and 'the man is dark'), consists in my opinion in the fact that in the first a concept is thought of as *determinate* and in the second it is the action of my *determining* the concept that is thought of. Hence you are quite right to say that in the *compound* concept the unity of the consciousness is given as *subjective*, but in the *composition* of concepts the unity of the consciousness is made as *objective*. That is, in the first the man should merely be *thought of* as dark (problematically represented); in the second he should be *apprehended* as such a man. Hence the question whether I can say without contradiction: 'the dark man (who is dark at one time) is pale (that is, he is pale, has blenched, at another time)'? My answer is no; since I transfer in this judgement the concept of the dark man to the concept of the not-dark man, while the subject is thought of as determinate through the first; con- ^{XI 334} sequently, since the subject would be both at the same time, it is self-contradictory. On the other hand, I could say of one and the same person *he is dark*, and also *this same person is not dark*, (namely, at another time, when he has become pale), since, in both judgements, only the *action* of *determining* is indicated and this is dependent on the conditions of experience and of time. You will also come across something about this in my Critique of Pure Reason, where I talk about the Law of Contradiction.

To what you say about your definition of intuition, that it is a thoroughly *determinate* representation with regard to a given multiplex, I have nothing further to mention, except that the thorough determination must be understood here objectively and not as found in the subject (since we cannot possibly know all the determinations of the object of an empirical intuition), for then the definition would not say more than: it is the representation of a single given thing. Now, although no compound *as such* can be given to us, and although we must always make the *composition* of the given multiplex ourselves, yet the composition, conceived as conformable to the object, cannot be arbitrary. Consequently, even though the compound cannot be given *a priori*, the form, in accordance with which alone the given multiplex can be compounded, must be given *a priori*. This is the mere subjectivity (sensibility) of the intuition, *a priori* indeed, but not thought, (since only the *composition* as action is a product of thought); it must rather be *given* in us (space and time); consequently it must be an *indi-*

vidual representation and not a concept (*representatio communis*).—It seems to me advisable not to linger a long time over the subtlest analysis of the elementary representations since they are sufficiently clarified by their usage in the sequel of the treatise.

As far as the question is concerned: can there not be actions incompatible with a natural order and which are yet prescribed by the moral law, I answer: indeed! namely a *determinate natural order* e.g. that of the present world: e.g. a courtier must recognise it as a duty to be at all times honest, even though he will not then long remain a courtier. But there is, in that type, only the form of *a natural order in general*; that is, the connection of actions as events according to *moral laws*, as with *natural laws*, merely looked at from the viewpoint *of their generality*; for this does not concern the particular laws of any nature.

XI 335

But I must conclude.—The sending of your manuscripts will be a pleasure to me. I will go through it alone and also together with *Schulz*, the Court Preacher.—Please thank Prof. *Jacob*[4] very much indeed for what he has sent me and also for the honour shown to me by the dedication.[11] Thank Magister *Hoffbauer*[12] too for sending his Analytic and say to both of them that I shall have the honour of answering their letters in the immediate future.—With best wishes for your happiness—I remain,

Your

I. Kant.

Königsberg,
3 July 1792.

Letter 17 (DIV)   *Königsberg 16 (17) October 1792*

To JACOB SIGISMUND BECK

XI 361

Highly esteemed friend,

The day before yesterday, 15 October, I packed your manuscript in grey paper, sealed it, signed it A.M.B.[13] and gave it to the mail for return, but, as I now see, too hastily. Through a failure of memory I thought that the appointed date for the return of your manuscript was the end of October instead of the end of November and, in my quickly made decision not to miss the departure of the first imminent post, I failed to check your letter again on this point; and since I found nothing important to notice in looking through the first sheets I surrendered your deduction of the categories and principles to its fate in good trust.

The mistake can, however, if you find it necessary, be repaired, if you send me by express post (unfranked, of course) those pages on which that deduction is to be found and which can be hastily copied out, and thus still receive my answer before the expiry of the time. In my judgement everything depends on this: since, in the empirical concept of the *compound*, composition can only be represented as given, not by means of the mere intuition and its apprehension, but rather through the *self-active connection* of the complex, given in intuition and to a consciousness (not in its turn empirical) in general, hence, this connection and its function must be subject in the mind to rules *a priori* xi 362 which constitute pure thought of an object generally (the pure concept of the understanding). The apprehension of the complex must be subordinate to this, insofar as it constitutes an intuition and also the condition of all possible empirical knowledge of what is compound or of what belongs to what is compound (i.e. wherein there is synthesis), which is stated by those fundamental principles. According to the commonly accepted notion, the representation of a compound as such, is subsumed as something given, under the representations of what is multiplex, which is apprehended. Thus, it does not belong completely, as it must, to spontaneity etc.

I was very much pleased by your insight into the importance of the physical question about the varying density of matter, which must be conceivable if one banishes all empty interstices as the explanation of the phenomenon, for it is very few who appear to have rightly understood even the question itself. I would, perhaps, place the way to solve this problem in the following fact: that attraction (universal, Newtonian attraction) is originally the same in all matter; it is only the repulsion in various materials that is different; and this constitutes the specific difference in density in these different materials. But this does lead, to a certain extent, to a circle from which I am unable to escape, and I must try further to understand myself better therein.

Your own method of solution will also not satisfy you, if you are willing to take the following fact into consideration. You say, namely: 'the effect which a small terrestrial body has on the whole world is infinitely small in comparison to that which the earth, by its attraction, has on it.' This should run: 'in comparison with that, which this small body exercises on another body, *equal* to or *smaller* than itself.' For, insofar as it attracts the whole earth, it will receive from the earth's resistance a movement (velocity) exactly equal to that which the earth's attraction gives to it by itself. Consequently, its velocity is twice as large as that which the body would receive if it had itself no gravitational attraction at all. The earth, however, by the resistance of the body which it attracts, has a velocity similarly twice as large as that which it would have received from the body alone if it had no gravitational attraction itself. But maybe xi 363 I do not completely understand your way of explanation and further elucidation would be very welcome to me.

Incidentally, if you could so shorten your extract—in such a way as not to damage its completeness, of course—so that your book could serve as the basis for lectures, it would be a great advantage to the publisher and also yourself, especially since the Critique of Practical Reason is there too. But I am apprehensive that the Transcendental Dialectic will take up a fair amount of space. However all this is left to your discretion and I am with true friendship and esteem,

Your

most devoted servant,

I. Kant.

Königsberg, 17 October 1792.

Letter 18 (DXVI)   *4 December 1792*

To JACOB SIGISMUND BECK

Since you allowed me, worthy man, in your letter of 10 XI 379
November a respite of four weeks for my answer,—a respite
which this letter will exceed by only a few days,—I don't
think that the accompanying little remarks will arrive too
late.—I must at this point remark in passing that, since I
cannot assume that the pages and lines of the transcript sent
me will correspond to those in the script you have, once you
have found the page of the transcript quoted, by means of
the initial words of a passage, distinguished here by quota-
tion marks ' ', you will easily find the corresponding pages
in your manuscript, because of the uniformity of the trans-
script.—For sending back to you by *ordinary* mail what has
been sent to me would delay my answer to you too long,
while sending the answer by *express* mail would be a little XI 380
too expensive; for your last letter with the manuscript cost
me exactly two Reichsthaler, an expense which the tran-
scriber could easily have reduced by $\frac{3}{4}$, if he had not taken
such heavy paper and if he had written more closely together.

P. 5: it is said of the division: 'If it is synthetic, then it
must necessarily be trichotomy.' But this is not uncondi-
tionally necessary, but only when the division occurs (i) *a
priori*, (ii) in accordance with concepts (not, as in mathematics, through construction of concepts). The regular polyhedron can be divided *a priori* into five different bodies,
while the concept of the polyhedron is revealed in the intuition. But from the mere concept of the polyhedron one
would not see even the possibility of such a body, far less its
possible manifoldness.

P. 7. (Where the discussion is about the reciprocal effect
of substances on each other and the analogy between the
reciprocal determination of concepts in disjunctive judgements with the reciprocal effect of substances on each other):

instead of the words 'The former hang together while they': 'the former constitute a whole with exclusion of several parts from it; in the disjunctive judgement' etc.

P.—8. Instead of the words at the end of the paragraph 'The *I think* must accompany all the representations, in the synthesis': 'can accompany'.

P.—17. Instead of the words 'an understanding whose pure *I think*': 'an understanding whose pure *I am*' etc. (for otherwise it would be a contradiction to say that its pure thought would be an intuition).

You see, dear friend, that my suggestions are of only small consequence. Furthermore, your representation of the deduction is correct. It is indeed true that explanations by means of examples would have relieved the understanding of many a reader; but the saving of space had also to be taken into account.

Herr *Eberhard*'s[8] and Herr *Garve*'s[14] opinion that Berkeleyan Idealism is identical with my Critical Idealism, which I could better call the Principle of the *Ideality* of Space and Time, does not deserve the least attention. For I speak of ideality, in respect of the *form* of the *representation*. But they make out of it ideality, in respect of the *matter*, i.e. of the *object* and is existence itself. Someone, however, under the assumed name of *Aenesidemus*,[15] has produced a still more radical scepticism, namely: that we cannot indeed know whether anything else (as object) corresponds to our representations at all; which may say about as much as: we do not know whether a representation is a representation (represents *something*). For representation signifies a determination in us which we relate to something else, the former taking the place, as it were, of the latter.

Concerning your effort to make intelligible the difference in densities (if one can make use of this expression) of two bodies, which both indeed completely fill their space: in my opinion, the moment of the acceleration of all earthly bodies must be accepted as equal between them, so that no difference will be met as between dx and dy. This I remarked in my previous letter. The quantity of the velocity of the one compared with that of the other, (i.e. their masses), can indeed be represented as unequal, when this problem is solved. Thus, mass in identical volume can be conceived, not in terms of *quantity of parts*, so to say, but in terms of *degree of specifically different parts*; whereby mass could have different magnitude, the speed of movement being exactly the same. For if mass depended on quantity of parts, all things would have to be conceived as originally equal, and consequently, when compounded into one and the same volume, they could only be thought as different in terms of empty interstices; which is contrary to the hypothesis.—Towards the end of the winter I shall communicate to you my efforts on this topic, undertaken during the composition of my *Metaphysical First Principles of Natural Science*, but which I rejected, before you start epitomising it. —For the benefit of your future extract from the *Critique of Judgement* I will send to you, in the immediate future, by mail, for your own personal use, a parcel containing the manuscript of my earlier introduction to the *Critique*. I rejected it, however, simply because it was disproportionately extensive for the text; but it still seems to me to contain much that contributes to a more complete insight into the concept of the purposefulness of nature.[16] For the benefit of your work I wanted also to advise your taking into consideration *Snell*'s,[17] but still more *Spazier*'s.[18] Treatises or Commentaries on this book.

I approve completely the title: *Explanatory extract from the critical writings of Kant. First Volume, containing the Critique of Speculative and Practical Reason*, which you propose giving your book.

I wish you furthermore the best success in this, as in all your undertakings, and I am, with respect and devotion,

Yours,
I. Kant.

Königsberg, 4 December 1792.

Letter 19 (DLI)   *Königsberg, 18 August 1793*

To Jacob Sigismund Beck

xi 426 I am sending you herewith, most worthy man, in accordance with my promises, the treatise intended previously as the Foreword to the *Critique of Judgement*, but rejected because of its extensiveness. I am sending it to you so that you may use this or the other form, according to your own discretion, for your concentrated extract from that book. Along with it, I am sending the specimen of it sent me through Court Preacher, *Schulz*.

The essential part of that Foreword (which may extend to about half the manuscript) examines the special and singular presupposition of our reason: that, in the multiplicity of its products, nature favoured—arbitrarily as it were and as the purpose of our comprehending faculty—accommodation to the limits of our faculty of judgement, by the simplicity and detectable unity of its laws; it favoured the presentation of this infinite variety of its kinds (species), according to a sure law of permanence, which makes it possible to group them together under a few generic concepts—not because we recognise this purposefulness as in itself necessary, but because we need it; and we are also thus justified in accepting it *a priori* and in making use of it, so long as it can suffice us. You will kindly forgive me if, with my age and many conflicting occupations, I have not been able to give to the specimen sent me the attention necessary to passing a considered judgement on it. But I can trust your own critical spirit in this. I remain furthermore, in all cases in which I can lend to your good wishes my whole fortune,

> Your most willing servant,
> I. Kant.

NOTES

I. Enquiry concerning the clarity of the principles of natural theology and ethics

Page 14

1. *Warburton, William, 1698–1779.* English critic, theologian and divine. Chaplain to George II and Bishop of Gloucester from 1760. Warburton's fame was established by his 1736 *Alliance between Church and State.* He defended the Anglican Church against the attacks of deists and freethinkers in his chief work: the *Divine legislation of Moses demonstrated on the principles of a religious deist,* 2 vols., 1737–41. Warburton was famous also as a critic and defender of Pope's *Essay on Man* and as the editor of Pope's *Works;* he also produced a Shakespeare edition in 1747. Warburton wrote a defence of revealed religion in his *View of Lord Bolingbroke's philosophy,* 1754. Hume's *Natural history of revealed religion* called forth his 1757 *Remarks . . .* produced in collaboration with his friend and biographer Richard Hurd.

Page 15

2. Kant refers to the *Confessions,* XI, 14, where St Augustine asks: 'For what is time? Who can easily and briefly explain it? Who can even comprehend it in thought or put the answer into words? Yet is it not true that in conversation we refer to nothing more familiarly or knowingly than time? And surely we understand it when we speak of it; we understand it also when we hear another speak of it. What then is time? If no one asks me, I know what it is. If I wish to explain it to him who asks me, I do not know. Yet I say with confidence that I know that if nothing passed away, there would be no past time; and if nothing were still coming there would be no future time; and if there were nothing at all, there would be no present time.' (Quoted from A. C. Outler's translation, *Library of Christian Classics,* vol. VII.)

Page 20

3. 'It is well known that the majority of Newtonians go still further than Newton himself and assert that bodies attract each other immediately at a distance (or, as they express it, through empty space).' Cf. A. Koyré, *Newtonian Studies,* London, 1965,

153

p. 149 ff. Koyré explains in Appendix C, pp. 149–63, 'Gravity an essential property of matter?' that Newton himself did not regard gravity as an 'innate, essential and inherent property of matter', and he points out that Newton (in a letter to Bentley in 1692) asked Bentley not to ascribe to him that Epicurean notion of 'attraction as action at a distance through vacuum without mediation' and described this concept as 'an utter absurdity'. Koyré argues that Newton's views in *Principia Mathematica* are not so explicit, and examines the development of Newton's views. As Kant points out, the followers of Newton had fewer scruples about the concept of 'attraction as action at a distance through vacuum without mediation'.

Page 22

4. *Sauvage*. It is difficult to know to whom Kant is referring. It is conceivable that the reference is to *François Boisier de Sauvages de la Croix, 1706–67*, a French botanist and doctor. He established his fame with a doctoral thesis entitled *L'amour peut-il être gueri par des remèdes tirés des plantes*. In 1730 he returned to Paris from Montpellier and published an important botanical-type classification of illnesses, *Traité des classes des maladies* (Paris, 1731). The *Nouvelle Biographie Générale* remarks on Sauvages: 'Comme médicin il était consulté de toutes partes: cependant ses vues eussent été plus sûres s'il avait eu moins de penchant pour certains systèmes, en particulier, pour celui de Stahl, touchant le pouvoir de l'âme sur le corps. . . .'

Page 26

5. *Crusius, Christian August, 1715–75*. German philosopher and theologian. Born at Leuna near Merseburg, Saxony, he was educated at Leipzig where he became Professor of Theology in 1750. Crusius was an opponent of the philosophy of Wolff. His most important works were the 1745 *Entwurf der nothwendigen Vernunftwahrheiten* and the 1747 *Weg zur Gewissheit und Zuverlässigkeit der menschlichen Erkenntnis*. It is in this latter work that Crusius lays down the supreme law that 'What cannot be imagined is false; and what cannot be imagined to be false is true.' From this Principle of Conceivability three subordinate Laws of Thought are deduced: *principium contradictionis, principium inseparabilium* and the *principium*

inconjungibilium. From these may be deduced further laws. Crusius also maintained that everything must be somewhere and somewhen; existence is defined as being anywhere and at any time; and from this he concludes that there is nothing which is not limited in its existence by time and space; even God is not excepted: time and space are accordingly abstractions which the intellect must distinguish in existence. Cf. also A. Marquardt, *Kant und Crusius.*

Page 34

6. *Hutcheson, Francis, 1694–1746.* Born at Drumalig, Co. Down, he studied philosophy, classics and theology at Glasgow University from 1710 to 1716. He opened a private academy in Dublin, and it was there that he published the four essays which established his fame: *Inquiry concerning beauty, order, harmony and design,* 1725, *Inquiry concerning moral good and evil, 1725, Essay on the nature and conduct of the passions and affections,* 1728, and *Illustrations upon the moral sense,* 1728. In 1729 Hutcheson returned to Glasgow as Professor of Moral Philosophy. Hutcheson's chief work was in moral philosophy. He was deeply influenced by Shaftesbury, whom he followed in opposing the thought of Hobbes and Mandeville, in drawing an analogy between beauty and virtue, in maintaining that benevolence is a fundamental aspect of human nature, and finally in maintaining that the criterion of a virtuous action is its tendency to promote the general well being. Hutcheson is generally regarded as the founder, with Shaftesbury, of the Moral Sense School of moral philosophy. Hutcheson ascribes to man a variety of senses, apart from the five external senses: (i) consciousness, by which man is aware of his own mind, (ii) a sense of beauty, (iii) a public sense (*sensus communis*) or 'a determination to be pleased with the happiness of others and to be uneasy at their misery', (iv) the moral sense or 'the moral sense of beauty in actions and affections, by which we perceive virtue or vice, in ourselves or others', (v) a sense of honour, and (vi) a sense of the ridiculous. The moral sense is the most important and pronounces immediately on the character of actions and affections, approving the virtuous and disapproving the vicious. God 'has made virtue a lovely form to excite our pursuit of it, and has given us strong affections to be the springs of each virtuous action'.

II. Concerning the ultimate foundation of the differentiation of regions in space

Page 36

1. *Boerhaave, Hermann, 1668–1738.* Dutch physician and distinguished professor of medicine. Born near Leyden, where he graduated in philosophy, he later studied medicine at Harderwyck. The remainder of his life was spent at the University of Leyden where he held the chairs of botany, medicine and chemistry. Boerhaave established the fame of Leyden University and, in particular, made its School of Medicine famous throughout Europe and indeed beyond. (Peter the Great took lessons from Boerhaave in 1715.) His principal works were the 1708 *Institutiones medicae*, the 1709 *Aphorismi de cognoscendis et curandis morbis* and the 1724 *Elementa Chemiae.*

2. *Buffon, George Louis Leclerc, Comte de, 1707–88.* French naturalist. Studied law at Dijon, making the acquaintance of Lord Kingston, with whom he toured Italy and England. 1735 Buffon published a translation of Hale's *Vegetable Statics* and in 1740 of Newton's *Fluxions.* In 1739 he became keeper of the Jardin du Roi and of the Musée Royale. Here Buffon began amassing the material for his *Histoire naturelle, générale et particulière* of which the first three volumes appeared in 1749. This work ran to forty-four volumes; the last eight volumes appeared posthumously.

3. '*the natural folding together in seeds*' is a translation of the phrase '*die Zusammenfaltungen der Natur in den Keimen*'. Kant's reference is to Buffon's *Histoire naturelle*, vol. II (1749) p. 373. The translation of the relevant passage by Smellie and Wood, in their Buffon's *Natural History*, London, 1812 (vol. III, pp. 50–1—*General history of Animals*, Chap. XI—'Of the expansion, growth and delivery of the foetus, etc.') runs as follows:

'This harmony in the position of the double parts of animals, is likewise apparent in vegetables. The branches push out small ramifications on each side; the small nerves in the leaves are equally disposed with regard to the principal nerve; and, if the symmetry appears to be less exact in vegetables than in animals, this proceeds only from its being more various, and because its limits are more extensive, and less precise. But the same order is easily recognisable; and the single and essential parts are perfectly distinct from those which are double; and it is evident that the latter derive their origin from the former.

'It is impossible to determine the form of these double parts before their expansion, or in what manner they are complicated, or what figure results from their position in relation to the single parts. The body of an animal, at the instant of its formation, unquestionably contains all the parts of which it ought to be composed: but the relative disposition of these parts is then very different from what afterwards appears. If we examine the expansion of a young leaf of a tree, we shall find that it is plaited on each side of the principal nerve; and that its figure, at this time, has no resemblance to that which it afterwards assumes. When we amuse ourselves with plaiting paper, in order to give it the form of a crown, of a boat, etc., the different plaits of the paper seem to have no resemblance to the figure which results from their expansion: we only perceive that the plaits are uniformly made in a certain order and proportion, and that, whatever is done on one side, is also done on the other. But, to determine the figures which may result from the expansion of any given number of folds, is a problem beyond the powers of geometry. The science of mathematics reaches not what immediately depends upon position. Leibnitz's art of "Analysis situs" does not yet exist; though the art of knowing the relations that result from the position of things would be, perhaps, more useful than that which has magnitude only for its object; for we have more occasion to be acquainted with form than with matter.'

4. '*At least it looks as if a certain mathematical discipline which he entitled in advance "Analysis situs"* . . . *was probably never more than a thing of the imagination.*' Kant's criticism seems not to be entirely grounded. See the fragments on a geometry of situation in Gerhardt, *Leibnizens mathematische Schriften*, vol. II, pp. 17–27; vol. V, pp. 178–83 (Berlin and Halle, 1849–63), translated in L. E. Loemker, *G. W. Leibniz: philosophical papers and letters*, Chicago, 1956, pp. 381–96. Cf. also Couturat, *La logique de Leibniz*, Paris, 1901, pp. 396 f.

Page 37

5. *Euler, Leonhard, 1707–83.* Swiss mathematician. Born in Basel, he graduated in 1723 from Basel where he studied geometry under Jean Bernoulli. In 1727 he turned to theology, oriental languages

and medicine. At the invitation of Catherine I, Euler went to St Petersburg where he became Professor of Physics in 1730; three years later he succeeded Bernoulli to the chair of mathematics. His health and eyesight suffered during his stay in Russia. In 1741 Euler went to Berlin at the command of Frederick the Great. Euler contributed prolifically to the Royal Prussian Academy and the Academy of St Petersburg. In 1766 he obtained permission to return to Russia. Soon afterwards Euler went blind and it was his two sons, Krafft and Lexell, who helped him continue his work. His output remained prolific until his death.

Euler's greatest achievements were in the field of mathematics, his major works being the 1748 *Introductio in analysin infinitorum*, the 1755 *Institutiones calculi differentialis* and the 1768–70 *Institutiones calculi integralis*. Euler also made important contributions to applied mathematics, astronomy, hydrodynamics, optics and acoustics. His *Lettres à une princesse d'Allemagne sur quelques sujets de physique et de philosophie*, 1768–72, cover these fields.

Page 39

6. 'There even exists a very noted characteristic of the products of nature . . . they may be in perfect agreement'. It has been pointed out by J. Handyside (in *Kant's Inaugural Dissertation and early writings on space*, Chicago, 1928) that the information given by Kant in this paragraph is rather simpler than the facts warrant. Handyside remarks: '. . . but the direction of turning is not always constant throughout a natural order of plants, and sometimes is reversed even in successive internodes of the same stem.' The same variations are to be found among molluscs: about 17 genera are sinistral; about 14 genera are dexteral; about 4 genera are indifferently sinistral or dexteral; there are about 200 species in which sinistral convolutions are found in predominantly dexteral genera.

Page 40

7. *Mariotte, Edmé, c. 1620–84*. French physicist. Spent most of his life in Dijon where he was Prior of St Martin-sous-Beaune. He was one of the first members of the Académie des Sciences, founded in Paris in 1666. The first volume of the *Histoire et mémoires de l'Académie*, 1733, contains many papers by Mariotte on various subjects: the motion of fluids, nature of colour, on the notes of the trumpet,

on the barometer, the fall of bodies, the recoil of guns, the freezing of water, etc. Mariotte's chief work was his *Essais de physique*, 1676–9. The second of the essays, *De la nature de l'air*, contains a statement of Boyle's law which Mariotte discovered independently. In 1717 the *Œuvres de Mariotte* appeared in two volumes in Leyden.

8. *Ulloa, Antonio de, 1716–95*. Spanish marine scientist. Trained for the navy, Ulloa entered the 'gardes-marins' in 1733. In 1735 he was chosen to accompany La Condamine, Bouguer and Godin to measure one degree of the meridian at the equator in South America. The geodesic operations began in 1736 in the area of Quito. Ulloa's scientific work was strictly an accompaniment only to his more conventional naval duties, but his main interests were, in the end, scientific rather than naval. His chief works were: *Relacion historica del viage a la America meridional*, Madrid, 1748; *Noticias americanas, entretenimientos physico-historicos sobre la America meridional y la septentrional oriental*, Madrid, 1772; and *Observation faite en mer d'une éclipse de soleil*, Cadiz, 1778.

9. *Borelli, Giovanni Alfonso, 1608–79*. Italian physiologist and physicist; Cartesian philosopher. Born in Naples, he became Professor of Mathematics at Messina in 1649 and at Pisa in 1656. In 1667 he returned to Messina, but was obliged to retire to Rome where he lived under the protection of Christina, Queen of Sweden. Borelli's best known work was the *De motu animalium*, 1680–81, in which he sought to explain the movements of animal bodies on mechanical principles. In an earlier work, *Del movimento della cometa apparsa il mese di decembre 1664*, published under the pseudonym Pier Maria Mutoli, he suggested the idea of parabolic paths. Borelli produced many astronomical works including the 1666 *Theorica mediceorum planetarum ex causis physicis deducta*, in which he considered the influence of the attraction on satellites of the planet Jupiter.

10. *Bonnet, Charles, 1720–93*. Swiss naturalist and philosopher. He was born in Geneva. Although the law was his profession, his real interest was natural science. In 1740 he sent a paper to the Academy of Sciences in which the existence of parthenogenesis was maintained. Two years later he discovered that caterpillars and butterflies breathe through pores. In 1743 Bonnet became a Fellow of the Royal Society. In 1754 appeared his famous *Recherches sur l'usage des feuilles dans les plantes*, in which he suggested that plants have powers of sensation and discernment. Failing eyesight

turned his attention to philosophy. His *Essai de psychologie* appeared in 1754 and in 1760 his *Essai analytique sur les facultés de l'âme*. Bonnet continued to produce scientific and philosophic works until his death at Genthod near Geneva. Bonnet's other works include *Considérations sur les corps organisés*, 1762, *Contemplation de la Nature*, 1764–5, *Palingénésie philosophique*, 1769–70.

Page 43

11. *'Entity of reason'*. The expression 'Gedankending' suggests, in this context, *'ens rationis'* and is thus translated 'entity of reason' rather than 'thing of the imagination',—the translation offered of 'Gedankending' as it occurs in the first paragraph.

III. On the form and principles of the sensible and intelligible world (Inaugural Dissertation)

Page 45

1. The edition printed by Johann Jakob Kanter (as reported by Weischedel) gives the date as 20 August. The last two lines in his edition read: Königsberg, at the expense of Johann Jakob Kanter.

Page 51

2. In §§ 18–19.

Page 56

3. *Adequate* is here used in the special sense of what Kant elsewhere called *Vollständigkeit*. For his doctrine on this matter see his *Die falsche Spitzfindigkeit der vier syllogistischen Figuren*, Königsberg, 1762, p. 29 ff. (Akademie-Ausgabe, II, 58 ff.)

Page 59

4. *Use* corrected from *end*—Kant under Errata.

5. Both printed versions of the Latin text had words equivalent to *because of freedom* after *present in it*, but these are rejected by Kant in the Errata to the version used for the Berlin Academy edition.

Page 61

6. *Is only given*—J. J. Kanter.

Page 64

7. i.e. *Time is a continuous quantity*—Adickes.

Page 65

8. *Anfangsgründe der hohern Mechanik, welche von der Bewegung fester Körper besonders die praktischen Lehren enthalten. Abgefasst von Abraham Gotthelf Kästner*, Göttingen, 1766. A second edition appeared in 1793—Adickes.

Page 67

9. *Namely movement* added by Kant under Errata.

Page 70

10. i.e. literally *filled up*.

Page 72

11. The second word *only* does not appear in the text of J. J. Kanter.

Page 73

12. ? *They are substrates for the intellect*—Adickes, and this is supported by the reading of the text in the edition by J. J. Kanter. See also § 7 (Akademie-Ausgabe, II, 394, l. 33).

13. Corrected by Kant under Errata from *This number itself is only a manifold*.

Page 75

14. For a discussion of the term *commercium* here translated by *interaction* see *Critique of Pure Reason* B260.

15. The reference is to Aristotle, *Prior Analytics*, II, 18, 66a, 16.

Page 79

16. *Que nous voyons toutes choses en Dieu*—Malebranche, *De la Recherche de la Vérité*, Book III, Part II, chapter heading to Chapter VI, translated as *nos omnia in deo videre* in the Latin version published at Geneva in 1691. So Adickes.

Page 82

17. Literally '*a Lydian stone*'.

Page 83

18. *When the subject* . . . J. J. Kanter's edition.

Page 84

19. A traditional proverb repeated in *Critique of Pure Reason*, B83, and first found in Polybius, xxxiii, 21; cf. Lucian *Demon.*, 28.

Page 85

20. *Lettres à une princesse d'Allemagne sur divers sujets de physique et de philosophie*, by Leonhard Euler, 3 vols., published anonymously 1768–72. The reference is probably to letters 92 and 93 of the German translation of the first two volumes published at Leipzig in 1769. The princess was the eldest daughter of the Margrave of Brandenburg-Schwedt. So Adickes.

Pages 89 and 90

21. The term *convenience* is here used rather in the sense of *harmony* or *being in harmony with*.

22. See above, note 20 to page 85.

IV. Selections from Kant's correspondence with Lambert, Sulzer, Mendelssohn and Herz

Page 93

1. *Lambert, Johann Heinrich, 1728–78.* Physicist, mathematician, astronomer and philosopher. Born in Mulhouse, Alsace. After a period as private tutor he settled in Berlin, editing *Ephemeris*. He received many favours from Frederick the Great and was elected a member of the Berlin Royal Prussian Academy. His chief philosophical work, *Neues Organon oder Gedanken über die Erforschung und Beziehung des Wahren und dessen Unterscheidung von Irrtum und Schein*, appeared in 1764. He there analyses the distinction between analytic and synthetic method, and attempts on account of the relation of a priori and a posteriori knowledge. Lambert did important work in mathematics, extending the logistical enquiries of Leibniz and producing work foreshadowing non-Euclidean geometry. Lambert formulated a theory, now named after him, used in the calculation of planetary paths. In his 1761 *Kosmologische Briefe über die Einrichtung des Weltbaues* Lambert developed a

theory of the structure of the universe. His 1760 *Photometria sive de mensura et gradibus lucis, colorum et umbrae* laid the foundations of an exact method of measuring light intensity. Lambert's other works include: *Pyrometrie*, 1779, *Insigniores orbitae cometarum proprietates*, 1761, and *Beiträge zum Gebrauch der Mathematik und deren Anwendung*, 1765–72. Cf. Baensch, *Lamberts Philosophie und seine Stellung zu Kant*, 1902.

Page 94

2. '*Acta Eruditorum*'. The first learned journal to appear in Germany was the *Acta Eruditorum Lipsiensia*. Founded in 1682 in Leipzig by Otto Mencke, it was a conscious imitation of the more famous *Journal des Savants*. It published articles on philosophy, physics, medicine, surgery, anatomy and philology. It ceased existence in 1782 after 117 volumes.

3. '*Bremische Beiträge*'. This journal, otherwise known as *Bremer Beiträge, neue Beiträge zum Vergnugen des Verstandes und Witzes*, first appeared in 1744 and was published by the so-called '*Bremer Beiträger*' or 'Bremen Contributors'. These included Gartner, Cramer, Rabener, the Schlegel brothers, Ebert and Gellert. The *Bremische Beiträge* was a literary journal set up in opposition to a journal published by a disciple of Gottsched; it represented a turn away from Gottsched's rationalism and championed a somewhat more liberal poetic and moral ideal. Special prominence was given to the fable and to satire.

4. *Gellert, Christian, 1715–69*. Poet and moralist. As a young man he was attached to the Gottsched circle; later he lectured on poetry and moral philosophy at Leipzig. His ethical lectures were published posthumously in 1770. His chief work, *Das Leben der schwedischen Gräfin von G* (1746) combined the family novel of Richardson with the traditional novel of adventure.

5. *Rabener, Gottlieb, 1714–71*. Satirical writer. He published the chief part of his prose satires in the *Bremische Beiträge*.

6. *Klopstock, Friedrich, 1724–1803*. German writer of great distinction. Studied in Jena and Leipzig where he became acquainted with the 'Bremen Contributors'. He published the first three stanzas of his *Messias* in the *Bremische Beiträge*. Initially an enthusiastic admirer of the French Revolution, Klopstock became disillusioned with the movement and gave expression to his disappointment in his latest works.

Page 96

7. '*Time is a subjective condition*': cf. *Inaugural Dissertation*, III §14.

Page 98

. 8. 'Theological difficulties which have rendered the doctrine of space a prickly one, especially since the time of Leibniz and Clarke. . . .': cf. *Philosophische Schriften von Leibniz*, vol. VII, p. 352f. (Gerhardt's edition).

Page 100

9. '*Phenomenology.*' Lambert refers to the second part of his 1764 '*Neues Organon . . .*' which was entitled '*Phenomenologie*'.

Page 101

10. *Haude- und Spenersche Zeitung:* a newspaper founded in 1740 in Berlin by A. Haude. Frederick the Great used the paper for political purposes and even wrote for it himself. Later J. K. Spener took the paper over and it became known as the *Haude- und Spenersche Zeitung*. It appeared under various names until 1938.

11. *Allgemeine deutsche Bibliothek.* A cultural journal founded in 1765 and published in Berlin. It ceased appearing in 1796.

12. *Göttingische Anzeige.* This journal was founded in 1739 and appeared under various names. Its major purpose was the review of all newly published books. Under the general editorship of Heyne, 1770–1813, it became an exclusively critical journal. It ceased at the end of Heyne's editorship in 1813.

13. *Leipziger gelehrte Zeitungen.* This learned journal, otherwise known as the *Neue Zeitungen von gelehrten Sachen*, was founded in Leipzig in 1715 and existed until 1792.

Page 102

14. *Sulzer, Johann Georg, 1720–79.* Philosopher and educationalist. The work for which Sulzer is chiefly remembered is his *Allgemeine Theorie der schönen Künste*, 2 parts, 1771–74. In this work he systematically treats the basic concepts and special problems of the different arts in particular and of aesthetics in general. His *Vermischte philosophische Schriften* appeared from 1773 until 1781 in two volumes.

Page 103

15. 'I have also attempted something of this kind, in that I have undertaken to answer the question, in what consists the physical and psychological difference between what we call a virtuous soul and one that is vicious. . . . But at the moment I cannot execute this work either.' The work referred to by Sulzer was his *Psychologische Betrachtungen über den sittlichen Menschen*, published in his *Vermischte philosophische Schriften* (1773–81) p. 282 f.

Page 104

16. *Mendelssohn, Moses, 1729–86.* Philosopher. Mendelssohn received a traditional Jewish education and was introduced to the thought of Maimonides. Shortly after 1743 Mendelssohn moved to Berlin, becoming private tutor to the family of Isaac Bernhardt. While in Berlin Mendelssohn made the acquaintance of Lessing. In 1749 Mendelssohn wrote his *Die Juden*, a work championing the notion of toleration. In 1755 Lessing published Mendelssohn's *Philosophische Gespräche* and in the same year they jointly wrote a famous essay *Pope, ein Metaphysiker!* In the years 1756–9 Mendelssohn became a leading spirit of Nicolai's *Bibliothek* and *Literaturbriefe*. In 1763 Mendelssohn won the prize offered by the Berlin Royal Prussian Academy for an essay on the application of mathematical proofs to metaphysics. Kant also competed and the 1763 *Enquiry concerning the clarity of the principles of natural theology and ethics* was Kant's unsuccessful effort. In 1763 Mendelssohn was granted the privilege of *Schutzjude*, entitling him to undisturbed residence in Berlin. Mendelssohn's 1767 *Phädon*, on the immortality of the soul, won him wide fame. Mendelssohn's life was devoted to the culture and emancipation of the Jews. In 1783 he produced a German translation of the Pentateuch and his *Jerusalem oder über religiöse Macht und Judenthum* of the same year contains a plea for toleration. Mendelssohn's own tolerant outlook is shown by his theory of the relativity of religions: that different nations need different religions, but that all are in some sense—a pragmatic sense—true. In 1785 Mendelssohn wrote his *Morgenstunde, oder über das Dasein Gottes*. Mendelssohn is generally regarded as the subject of Lessing's *Nathan, der Weise*. He was the grandfather of the composer Mendelssohn-Bartholdy.

17. *Herz, Marcus, 1747–1803.* Doctor and philosopher. In 1770 Herz began practising medicine in Berlin. He acted as respondent

in Kant' 1770 Inaugural Dissertation, and in the following year, 1771, published a popularised version of Kant's Dissertation, the *Betrachtungen aus der spekulativen Weltweisheit*. It was to Herz that Kant first revealed his plan of writing the *Critique of Pure Reason* (cf. Kant's Letter to Herz, 21 February 1772, No. 5 (LXV). Herz's chief works include *Versuch über den Geschmack*, 1776 and *Versuch uber den Schwindel*, 1786.

Page 105

18. 'In the second edition of my philosophical writings . . .' Mendelssohn is here referring to his *Philosophische Schriften, verbesserte Auflage* (Berlin 1771), Part I, p. 247 ff.

19. *Shaftesbury, Antony Ashley Cooper, 3rd Earl, 1671–1713*. Born at Exeter House, London, Shaftesbury was brought up by his grandfather and early entrusted to the tutorship of Locke. After a period of foreign travel, private study and political activity, Shaftesbury was compelled by bad health to retire to a life of seclusion devoted to philosophy. He divided his time between Holland (where he made the acquaintance of Le Clerc, Bayle and Furley), London, and his country residence in Somerset. Shaftesbury died in Naples, 1713, whither he had fled on account of his health. Shaftesbury is famous as the author of *Characteristics of men, manners, opinions and times*, 1711, a collection of works, including his 1699 *Inquiry concerning virtue*, his 1708 *Letter on enthusiasm*, his 1709 *Sensus communis, an essay on the freedom of wit and humour*, the 1709 *The moralists* and the 1710 *Soliloquy, or advice to an author*. The third volume contains his *Miscellaneous reflexions*. Shaftesbury is generally regarded as the founder, with Hutcheson, of the moral sense school. According to Shaftesbury, to be good or virtuous means to direct one's inclinations to the good or well-being of the species or system of which one is a part. Virtue is thus the subordinating of the egoistic to the altruistic affections, though Shaftesbury maintains that both affections are harmoniously ordered in all but perverted natures. Man, according to Shaftesbury, has a faculty which apprehends the beauty, goodness, virtue or harmony of a good action, and this faculty is called the moral sense. Shaftesbury exercised an enormous influence on German writers and philosophers; Kant certainly owes an intellectual debt to him.

20. 'You number Lord Shaftesbury among those who follow Epicurus, at least at a distance.' cf. Inaugural Dissertation, II, § 9.

Page 106

21. 'Page 15. "What does the little word after mean" etc.' Cf. Inaugural Dissertation, III, § 14.

Page 107

22. 'Side 17. I do not understand how you find a vicious circle in this manner of conceiving time.' Cf. Inaugural Dissertation, III, § 14, No. 5.

23. 'Side 23.' Cf. Inaugural Dissertation, III, Corollary.

Page 110

24. 'I have learned with pleasure that you are about to give to the press a treatise on the nature of speculative knowledge.' Kant is referring to the popularisation by Herz of the Inaugural Dissertation published in Königsberg in 1771. Cf. note 17 to page 104 above.

Page 113

25. *Malebranche, Nicolas, 1638–1715.* French philosopher of the Cartesian School. He was born at Paris, deformed and constitutionally feeble. He studied theology in the Sorbonne and in 1660 joined the Congregation of the Oratory. In 1664, having read Descartes' *Traité de l'Homme*, Malebranche devoted himself to a detailed study of Descartes' philosophy. In 1674 Malebranche published his *De la recherche de la vérité . . .*, following this with a series of controversial and speculative works. Malebranche was interested also in mathematics and physics, being made a member of the Académie des Sciences in 1699. Malebranche's other works include: *Conversations métaphysiques et chrètiennes,* 1677; *Traité de la nature et de la grace,* 1680; *Méditations chrètiennes et métaphysiques,* 1683; *Traité de morale,* 1684; *Entretiens sur la métaphysique et sur la religion,* 1688; and *Traité de l'amour de Dieu,* 1697.

26. Crusius. See page 26, note 5.

27. On the preformation system compare the judgement of Kant in the *Critique of Pure Reason*, B, pp. 167–8: 'A middle course may be proposed between the two above mentioned, namely, that the categories are neither *self-thought* first principles *a priori* of our knowledge nor derived from experience, but subjective dispositions of thought, implanted in us from the first moment of our existence, and so ordered by our Creator that their employment is in

complete harmony with the laws of nature in accordance with which experience proceeds—a kind of *preformation-system* of pure reason. Apart, however, from the objection that on such an hypothesis we can set no limit to the assumption of predetermined dispositions to future judgments, there is this decisive objection against the suggested middle course, that the *necessity* of the categories, which belongs to their very conception, would then have to be sacrificed. The concept of cause, for instance, which expresses the necessity of an event under a presupposed condition, would be false if it rested only on an arbitrary subjective necessity, implanted in us, of connecting certain empirical representations according to the rule of causal relation. I would not then be able to say that the effect is connected with the cause in the object, that is to say, necessarily, but only that I am so constituted that I cannot think this representation otherwise than as thus connected. This is exactly what the sceptic most desires. For if this be the situation, all our insight, resting on the supposed objective validity of our judgments, is nothing but sheer illusion; nor would there be wanting people who would refuse to admit this subjective necessity, a necessity which can only be felt. Certainly a man cannot dispute with anyone regarding that which depends merely on the mode in which he is himself organised.' (Kant, *Critique of Pure Reason*, translated Kemp Smith, pp. 174-5.)

Page 115

28. *Breslauische Zeitung*. A cultural and later a political journal founded in 1742. It ceased appearing in 1819.

29. *Schulz, Johann, 1739-1805*. The later commentator of the *Critique of Pure Reason*. The commentaries are contained in two major works: *Erläuterungen über des Herrn Prof. Kant Kritik der reinen Vernunft*, Königsberg, 1784, and *Prüfung der Kantischen Kr. d. r. V.*, 2 vols., 1789, 1792. The former of these two commentaries is especially important in that it was published with Kant's own approval. (There are various orthographies of Schulz's name: e.g. Schultz, Schultze, Schulze.)

Page 116

30. 'An objection . . . which Herr Lambert made against me.' The objection is contained in Lambert's letter to Kant, 13 October 1770 (1/LVII).

Page 117

31. *Baumgarten, Alexander Gottlieb, 1714–62.* Philosopher. Baumgarten became professor of philosophy at Frankfurt a. Oder in 1740. His *Metaphysica* appeared in 1739 and was used by Kant in his lectures. The book is written from a Wolffian standpoint. The following year saw the appearance of his *Ethica Philosophica.* Baumgarten's *magnum opus* was his *Aesthetica*, 1750–8. In this work he systematically developed that branch of philosophy concerned with the beautiful and was the first to use the term 'aesthetics', on the ground of his definition of beauty as perfection apprehended through the senses.

32. '*Metaphysica*'. Kant used Baumgarten's 1739 *Metaphysica* in accordance with the ban, imposed by the Prussian government, on 'free'—i.e. original—lectures. University teachers were obliged to read from, and comment upon, some recognised classic in their given field. A special exception was made in the case of Kant's anthropological lectures, since this was a field in which a 'classic' text did not exist.

Page 118

33. 'Macbride's systematic pharmaceutics . . .' Kant's reference is to Macbride's *Introduction to theoretical and practical surgery,* the German translation of which appeared at Leipzig in 1773.

Page 120

34. '*Platner's Anthropology*'. Kant is referring to Platner's *Anthropologie für Ärzte und Weltweise* published in two volumes at Leipzig in 1772–3. Ernst Platner, 1744–1818, studied at Leipzig where he successively held the chairs of medicine and in 1780 of physiology. He later turned to philosophy, becoming in 1801 *extraordinarius* for philosophy and then *ordinarius* in 1811. Apart from the work referred to, Platner's chief works were: *Philosophische Aphorismen*, 1776–82, *Questiones physiologicae*, 1794, and *Lehrbuch der Logik und Metaphysik*, 1795.

Page 121

35. *Friedlander, David, 1750–1834.* Jewish writer and close friend of Moses Mendelssohn; he was a strong advocate of religious toleration and the emancipation of the Jews.

Page 122

36. *Garve, Christian, 1742–98*. Philosopher. Professor in Leipzig. One of the most famous 'popular' writers of the Enlightenment. He launched a strong attack on Kant's categorical imperative in his five volume collection of Essays on various social, ethical and literary topics: *Versuche über verschiedene Gegenstände aus der Moral, Literatur, und dem gesellschaftlichen Leben* (1792–1802). Garve also translated Aristotle's Ethics and Politics, subjoining a review of the history of morals, with an especially thorough examination of the Kantian Doctrine: *Übersicht der vornehmsten Principien der Sittenlehre von dem Zeitalter des Aristoteles an bis auf unsere Zeiten* (1798).

37. 'It was with pleasure that I observed the purity of expression, the pleasantness of the style and the subtlety of the remarks in your book on the difference of taste.' The book referred to by Kant is Herz's *Versuch über den Geschmack und die Ursachen seiner Verschiedenheit*, Leipzig, 1776.

Page 125

38. *Tetens, Johannes Nikolaus, 1736–1807*. Philosopher and psychologist. Became professor in Kiel in 1776 and after 1769 lived in Copenhagen. Tetens was the first philosopher to give to the faculty of feeling a status coordinate with that of understanding and will. He included in feeling not only pleasure and pain, but also sensuous impressions, and the impressions which the mind produces on itself. Kant refers in this passage to Tetens' chief work: *Philosophische Versuche über die menschliche Natur und ihre Entwicklung*, 2 vols., 1776–7.

39. *Zedlitz, Karl Abraham, Freiherr von, 1731–93*. Zedlitz's chief claim to fame is the fact that Kant dedicated the *Critique of Pure Reason* to him. In addition, he is remembered for his important and lasting services to education in Prussia. He was Minister of Justice in 1770 and in 1771 he became Minister of Culture and Education.

Page 126

40. *Breitkopf, Johann Georg*. Publisher in Leipzig. On the appearance of Kant's paper on *The Races of Mankind* Breitkopf wrote to Kant suggesting that the theme be developed at length in a new book. Kant's reply is contained in the letter to Breitkopf dated

1 April 1778. Breitkopf was one of the most successful publishers of his time. The company still exists.

41. 'It cannot be other than very pleasant for me to comply with your request, especially since the intention is one that stands in relation to my own interest.' Kant is referring to the fact that Herz had applied to him for transcripts of his lectures on Logic and Metaphysics.

Page 127

42. *Kraus, Christian Jacob, 1753–1807.* A pupil of Kant's and later, as professor of moral and political philosophy in Königsberg, one of Kant's closest friends.

43. *Joel, Aaron, born 1749.* Joel studied in Königsberg and in 1778 left to practise medicine in Berlin.

Page 129

44. *Biester, Johann Erich, 1749–1816.* From the year 1777 Biester was secretary in the ministry of von Zedlitz; he later published the *Berlinische Monatschrift.* Like von Zedlitz, Biester was introduced to the Kantian philosophy through Herz's lectures. In a letter to Kant, 11 April 1779, Biester wrote: 'This week Herz began, after a pause, psychology, which he intends completing without interruption in three months. Our Minister . . . does not miss a single lecture. Sometimes he invites Kraus to a philosophic conversation with him. In the reflected light of these two we recognise your light.' (Quoted from Cassirer's edition of Kant's works.)

45. *Dr. Heintz.* Lawyer and later professor *extraordinarius* in Königsberg.

V. Selections from Kant's correspondence with Beck

Page 131

1. *Beck, Jacob Sigismund, 1761–1840.* German philosopher. Born in Danzig, Beck was educated at Königsberg. He became *Privatdozent* in philosophy at Halle in 1791 and professor in 1799 at Rostock. Beck devoted himself to the criticism and explanation of the Kantian philosophy. While at Halle, Beck produced his *Erläuternder Auszug aus Kants kritischen Schriften,* 1793, a work widely used as a compendium of Kantian thought. Beck often

attempts to explain away certain contradictions within the Kantian system by arguing that Kant often uses ordinary language for the sake of greater intelligibility, and that it is the ordinary language which produces the appearance of contradiction. Beck maintained that the real meaning of Kant is idealism: viz. that because knowledge of objects outside the domain of consciousness is impossible, nothing positive remains when the subjective element is removed. Apart from the three-volume '*Erläuternder Auszug*...', 1793–6, Beck's chief work was the *Grundriss der kritischen Philosophie*, 1796. Cf. also Dilthey, *Acht Briefe Kants an J.S.B.* in *Archiv für die Geschichte der Philosophie*, 1889; Pötschel, *Beck und Kant*, 1910.

2. 'It was very pleasant for me to receive the news of your entering your new career . . . .' Kant refers to the fact that Beck, having studied in Königsberg, became a *Privatdozent* at Halle in 1791.

Page 132

3. '. . . the subsistence based on the mere holding of seminars is very precarious . . .' A *Privatdozent* is financially dependent on the number of students he is able to attract to his courses; the position is not a salaried one, and it was normal for young University teachers to supplement their meagre and uncertain earnings by school teaching.

4. *Jacob, Ludwig Heinrich, 1759–1827*. Kantian philosopher who attacked Mendelssohn's proofs of the existence of God, from the critical viewpoint in his '*Prüfung der Mendelssohn'schen Morgenstunden*, Leipzig, 1786. Prof. Jacob was also the publisher of the '*Philosophischen Annalen*'.

Page 133

5. *Prof. Klügel:* Professor of mathematics in Königsberg.

6. *Hartknoch, Johann Friedrich, 1740–89*. Book merchant in Riga and Mitau. Hartknoch was the publisher of not only Kant, but also Herder and Hamann. The company of booksellers and publishers existed until 1879.

7. *Kästner, Abraham Gotthelf, 1719–1800*. Mathematician and composer of epigrams. In 1746 he became professor of mathematics in Leipzig and ten years later in Göttingen. He published a history of mathematics and a work on the principles of mathe-

matics. Kästner's fame is perhaps greater as a writer of epigrams and as a member of the Gottsched Circle.

Page 135

8. *'Eberhardt's Magazine.'* The *Philosophische Magazin* was edited by Eberhardt from 1788 until 1792. Johann August Eberhardt, 1739–1809, was a disciple of Wolff and an opponent of Kant. He was a professor of philosophy at Halle, and directed attacks against Kant in the *Philosophische Magazin*, particularly in the volumes for 1788 and 1789. These attacks led Kant to write a polemical paper *Über eine Entdeckung nach welcher, alle neue Kritik der Vernunft durch eine ältere entbehrlich gemacht werden soll*, 1790. Cf. on the subject of Kant's dispute with Eberhardt: Feuber *Der philosophische Streit zwischen Kant und Eberhardt*, Giessen, 1894.

9. *'Tübinger gelehrte Zeitung'*. The reference is probably to the *Tübingsche gelehrte Anzeigen*, 1783–1802, a learned journal published in Tübingen, although, according to Salomon's *Zeitungswesen*, a journal entitled *Tübinger gel. Zeitung* did appear from 1735–40.

10. *Reinhold, Karl Leonard, 1758–1823.* Kantian philosopher. Reinhold was the author of *Briefe über die kantischen Philosophie*, 1786–87, which contributed much to spreading the ideas of Kant. In 1787 Reinhold became professor of philosophy at Jena; and he was responsible for making Jena a central point for the study of Kant, and the *Jena allgemeine Literaturzeitung* (founded 1785) became the most influential organ of Kantianism. The work referred to by Kant is Reinhold's 1789 *'Versuch einer neuen Theorie des menschlichen Vorstellungsvermögens.'* In this work he attempts to give a new basis to critical idealism by examining the conception of mental representation, and analysing this notion in terms of a representing subject, and a represented object. The attempt was unsuccessful and Reinhold later repudiated the analysis. His *Elementarphilosophie*, 1792, established his law of Consciousness, according to which subject and object are always related to each other and as such must always remain unknown. Schopenhauer adopted this law. In addition to the works referred to, Reinhold was the author of *Über das Fundament des philosophischen Wissens*, 1791, and *Über die Paradoxien der neuesten Philosophie*, 1799.

Page 144

11. 'Please thank Prof. Jacob very much indeed for what he has

sent me and also the honour shown to me by the dedication', cf. Jacob's letter to Kant (*Kants gesammelte Schriften*, Acad. Edition, XI, p. 305). Jacob in this letter (No. CDLXX) writes: 'I assume that you have received and kindly accepted the copy of the new edition of my textbook, which I have been so free as to dedicate to you.'

12. *Hofbauer, Johann Christian*, was important for applying the Kantian philosophy to the field of law. In 1792 his *Analytik der Urteile und Schlüsse* appeared in Halle, and it is to this work that Kant makes reference.

13. 'A.M.B.' These letters are perhaps an abbreviation for 'An Magister Beck'.

Page 148

14. Garve: cf. note 36 to page 122.

15. *Aenesidemus.* This was the pseudonym assumed by *Gottlob Ernst Schulze*, 1761–1833. Schulze was professor first at Helmstedt and from 1810 at Göttingen. His chief criticism of Kant consisted in the assertion that there must be a causal relationship between experience and that which constitutes the basis of experience. He was the teacher of Schopenhauer. The reference made by Kant is to Schulze's pseudonymously published *Aenesidemus oder über die Fundamente der von dem H. Prof. Reinhold in Jena gelieferten Elementarphilosophie*, 1792. Cf. note 10 on Reinhold.

Page 149

16. 'For the benefit of your future extract from the *Critique of Judgement* I will send to you in the immediate future by mail for your own personal use a parcel containing the manuscript of my earlier introduction to the *Critique*. I rejected it, however, simply because it was disproportionately extensive for the text; but it still seems to me to contain much that contributes to a more complete insight into the concept of the purposefulness of nature.' The 'earlier introduction' was published in extracts by Beck under the title of *Über Philosophie überhaupt, zur Einleitung in die Kritik der Urteilskraft* and appears in Cassirer's edition of Kant's Works, vol. V, pp. 177–231.

17. *Snell, Friedrich Wilhelm Daniel, 1761–1827.* Born in Dachsenhausen, Snell became teacher of mathematics in Giessen in 1784. From 1789 he was active at the University of Giessen, eventually becoming Ordinarius for mathematics and in 1805 for history.

His writings were chiefly mathematical and philosophical. He was the author of *Darstellung und Erläuterung der kantischen Kritik der ästhetischen Urteilskraft*, Mannheim, 1791.

18. *Spazier, Johann Gottlieb Karl, 1761–1805.* Writer and song composer. He studied philosophy and theology at Halle and Göttingen, and for a while was a teacher in Dessau and later professor in Giessen. In 1791 he became a teacher of German language and fine arts in Berlin, and in 1792 he founded the *Berlinische musikalische Zeitung*. Spazier, who published various works of a theological, philosophical and musical nature, was the author of *Über Kants Kritik der Urteilskraft*.

INDEX OF NAMES

INDEX OF SUBJECTS